THE CALL TO HOLINESS

MARTIN PARSONS

THE
CALL TO HOLINESS

Spirituality in a Secular Age

Darton Longman and Todd

First published in 1974
by Darton Longman and Todd Ltd
85 Gloucester Road, London SW7 4SU

Printed in Great Britain in 1974 by
The Anchor Press Ltd and bound by
Wm Brendon & Son Ltd, both of Tiptree, Essex

ISBN 0 232 51288 4

Contents

1	The Starting Point	9
2	Some Basic Assumptions	16
3	Holiness: What Is It?	27
4	Holiness: How Does It Show?	34
5	Motives for Holy Living	43
6	The Experience of Holiness	53
7	The Means of Grace	65
8	The Urge to Evangelize	74
9	The Way Forward	85
	Books for Further Reading	96

Preface

When I gave my first address some fifty years ago, the leader of the Bible Class I attended took me by the arm and, after words of encouragement, said : 'If an older man may give you a word of advice, stick to your simplicity'. I do not suppose I have always succeeded, but it has certainly been my aim to follow that precept, and this book is no exception.

It was this same elder brother in Christ, John L. Oliver, who taught me Sunday by Sunday the meaning of Christian discipleship, and – more important still – who showed me in his own consecrated life the meaning of holiness. It was from him I learned that the more dedicated a man is to God, the more truly human he becomes. My gratitude to him is unbounded.

Many others have taught me the same, but the earliest impressions remain the strongest. I cannot begin to mention all those who have set before me the Call to Holiness, whether by example, personal counsel, public teaching or the written word. The short list of books for further reading in no way represents the extent of my indebtedness to very many writers, preachers and personal friends.

Yet what is here written is my own, and no one else can be held responsible. Where my views differ from others, I have tried to write with charity. I have endeavoured, as I explain, to let the Bible be my supreme guide. Except where stated otherwise, all quotations are from the Jerusalem Bible, a translation which I find helpful.

It goes without saying that none of us can shake off the influences under which we live and move and have our being. To that extent what I have written about holiness represents a well-defined tradition within the Church. I do not feel this needs any apology : we all have our distinctive insights into Christian doctrine. We can learn much from others, but each of us must bear witness in his own way to what makes him tick. This is what I have tried to do.

Locking, 1974   *Martin Parsons*

Chapter One

The Starting Point

Christianity early came to be known as the Way. Saul of Tarsus on the road to Damascus had letters with him 'that would authorize him to arrest and take to Jerusalem any followers of the Way, men or women, that he could find' (Acts 9.2). From other references in the Acts we can see that it was something of a technical term. We do not know how it originated, but it suggests that the followers of Jesus had adopted a certain manner of life which singled them out. Not only this, but they also appeared to be a group of people on the road, pilgrims who marched forward with set purpose. They knew where they were going. There was indeed a connection between their way of life and the destination to which they were moving. They were followers of one who had said : 'I am the Way, the Truth and the Life. No one can come to the Father except through me' (John 14.6). They were pressing towards the mark through Christ who is the Way. Their only hope of reaching God was through Jesus Christ, 'for there is only one God, and there is only one mediator between God and mankind, himself a man, Christ Jesus, who sacrificed himself as a ransom for them all' (1 Tim. 2.5,6). They came through him who is the Way, and his way of life became theirs. It was the way of holiness.

To some it may seem strange to speak of holiness in the times in which we live, and to write a book about it a somewhat bizarre undertaking. Holiness suggests a life which is a little remote from reality. We picture either a genuinely

good person, who because of his goodness is cut off from hi
fellow-men, or some sort of a Holy Joe who at best is a bi
of a crank, and at worst a downright humbug. And all thi
in a world facing problems of over-population, dire poverty
international tension, the breakdown of marriage and famil
life, and the possibility of complete moral anarchy. Is i
realistic to claim anyone's attention to the question o
personal holiness? Are there not bigger things to talk about

The fact is that mankind has lost its way. We do no
know where we are going, and life, far from being a pilgrimage, is more like a treadmill. But when I say that mankind
has lost its way I am not announcing a new discovery. I
was into just such a world that Jesus came. He came t
be the Way. Men did not want him. The Way he lived
and the Way he preached, were too demanding, and the
nailed him to a cross. But that cross has become the starting
point of the Way, for it was there that the one mediato
between God and mankind sacrificed himself as a ransom
for all. 'He died to make men holy.' There were plenty
of wrongs to be righted in the days of Christ. His method
was to choose men – only a few at first – and to change
them at the centre, to make them holy. He showed them
in his own life what holiness could be like. Jesus of Naza-
reth simply does not fit into any of the popular ideas of
holiness. He was not 'pi', or remote, or austere. No one
could call him a crank or a hypocrite. He was strong, and
true, and all love. No disciple of his from that day till
now has ever claimed to reach his standards, but that has
been their aim. The beauty of holiness has been seen, and
it has proved to be a revolutionary force. To this day there
is no argument so powerful, and no influence so persuasive,
as that of a holy life.

'The Way of Holiness' is a direct quotation from Isaiah
35.8 (N.E.B.). The passage from there to the end of the
chapter depicts a highway through the wilderness. It is a

most fitting description of the straight and safe pathway of the will of God through the desert of life. That way Jesus went, and along that same way he brings many sons to glory (Heb. 2.10). Of this Way Isaiah says, 'the unclean may not travel by it'. No comment of mine on those words could equal the words of Paul : 'With promises like these made to us, dear brothers, let us wash off all that can soil either body or spirit, to reach perfection of holiness in the fear of God' (2 Cor. 7.1). 'And fools shall not err therein' (R.S.V.), which could mean that even people without great wisdom can be guided safely along the highway of the will of God. It is a most important truth. Holiness has nothing to do with being clever. 'No lion will be there nor any fierce beast roam about it.' This is not quite the same as the picture given in the New Testament of 'your enemy the devil prowling round like a roaring lion, looking for someone to eat' (1 Pet. 5.8). But Christian in *The Pilgrim's Progress*, while he saw, and feared, the lions ahead of him, found, when he reached them, that they were chained. That is a true account of the dangers to be met on the Way of Holiness. 'But the redeemed will walk there, for those Yahweh has ransomed shall return.' The Christian redemption, through Christ crucified, is the New Testament basis of holy living. Finally, 'They will come to Zion shouting for joy, everlasting joy on their faces; joy and gladness will go with them, and sorrow and lament be ended.' The Way of Holiness is the way of abounding and infectious joy. This is an aspect of our subject which needs stressing. Why is there so little of the joy of the Lord in much of our Christianity?

The starting point of the Way of Holiness is the cross of Christ. I use the expression not simply to signify a historic happening, still less to concentrate on the events of Good Friday as if Jesus were still dead, but to mean the great saving act of God when Jesus died and rose again.

It is the living Christ, who suffered and died and rose again, whom we meet in the glad experience of conversion. In the words of Canon Max Warren :

'What is vital to the conversion experience is the personal encounter with Jesus Christ, a personal encounter which issues in personal commitment. May God save us from ever compromising in our ministry by allowing any one for whom we are responsible to get away with being "very religious" and missing the heart of religion which is the personal knowledge of the love of God. That personal knowledge can only be encompassed in a personal encounter. That is what we mean by the conversion experience.'*

If ever a man was 'very religious' it was John Wesley in his Oxford days. He and his fellow-members of the Holy Club lived a life of strict discipline according to the rules of the Church, and their asceticism, devotional practices and philanthropic activities marked them out from others, and produced the nickname of Methodists. Yet at this time, and subsequently after his ordination, and during missionary service in Georgia, he had nothing of what the Bible calls the joy of salvation. When he returned to England in 1738 he doubted whether he was a Christian at all. His later assessment, looking back, was that he had the faith of a servant, but not the faith of a son. What happened on May 24th, 1738, is well known. Listening to the reading of Luther's Preface to the Epistle to the Romans, 'I felt my heart strangely warmed. I felt I did trust in Christ, Christ alone, for salvation, and an assurance was given to me, that He had taken away my sins, even mine, and saved me from the law of sin and death'. What are perhaps less well known are these further words written in his journal that day.

* *The Sevenfold Secret*, S.P.C.K.

12

They show where his confidence had been up till then. 'By my continued endeavour to keep his whole law, inward and outward, I was persuaded that I should be accepted of him.' This conversion of a good and religious man, from confidence in his own goodness to faith in Christ alone, was the inspiration of all his subsequent ministry.

Not less significant in its effects on a world-wide scale was the conversion of Charles Simeon. As a godless young undergraduate from a worldly home he learned with dismay that it was the rule of his college, King's College, Cambridge, that he should receive Holy Communion at half-term, and again at Easter. Knowing that he was completely unready, he set about preparing himself. Books about the Christian's duties only plunged him into despair. At last he obtained a copy of a book by Bishop Wilson on the Lord's Supper, and there learned the truth of Christ's atoning death. He told later of 'the gradual manifestations of God's unbounded mercy to me, till on Easter-day I was enabled to see that all my sins were buried in my Redeemer's grave'. He awoke that morning with the words ringing in his mind : 'Jesus Christ is risen today! Hallelujah!' 'From that hour', he said, 'peace flowed in rich abundance into my soul; and at the Lord's Table in our Chapel I had the sweetest access to God through my blessed Saviour.' That was in 1779, and for over half a century he continued a ministry in Cambridge which brought new life to the whole Church.

Stories of conversions, some dramatic and some very ordinary, some of famous people and some of people quite unknown, some sudden and some not so sudden, could be multiplied indefinitely. For all the varieties of religious experience, there was always what Max Warren refers to as a personal encounter with Jesus Christ. Through this encounter people were brought to an assurance of their acceptance with God and dedicated their lives to his service. Always there is a once-and-for-allness about conversion.

Sometimes well-meaning people will use such expressions as 'half-converted', perhaps from fear of appearing arrogant. Or they will speak of the need to be converted, or re-converted, every day. We can understand what they mean. But properly understood conversion is a change of status, an entering into a new sphere. It is as much an historic event as baptism. No one would suggest that we need to be baptized every day, or that it is possible to be only half-baptized!

No better account of the conversion experience is to be found in any literature, apart from the Bible, than John Bunyan's description of Christian losing his burden 'So I saw in my dream, that just as Christian came up with the cross, his burden loosed from off his shoulders, and fell from off his back, and began to tumble, and so continued to do, till it came to the mouth of the sepulchre, where it fell in, and I saw it no more. Then was Christian glad and lightsome, and said, with a merry heart, "He hath given me rest by his sorrow, and life by his death".' Going back further in history we come across another moving account. Thomas Bilney was influenced by Cambridge companions to read the New Testament. 'And at the first reading, as I well remember, I chanced upon this sentence of St Paul (O most sweet and comfortable sentence to my soul!). "It is a true saying and worthy of all men to be embraced, that Christ Jesus came into the world to save sinners; of whom I am chief" (1 Tim. 1.15). This one sentence, through God's instruction and inward working, which I did not then perceive, did so exhilarate my heart, being before wounded with the guilt of my sins, and being almost in despair, that immediately I felt a marvellous comfort and quietness, insomuch that my bruised bones leaped for joy.' The story of how Bilney led Hugh Latimer to a like experience, by the novel method of asking him to hear his confession, is well known.

What more need be said? The personal encounter with

Jesus Christ, which issues in personal commitment, is always the beginning. But it is only a beginning. From that moment we are pledged to walk the Way of Holiness. I cannot accept myself that there are two classes of Christians, 'the normal life of the man who does his duty and says his prayers, and the higher, more spiritual, more devoted life'. That was the deduction of Canon James Hannay as a result of reading the devotional writings of Bishop Handley Moule.* But Bishop Moule would have deplored such an inference. He taught that the call to holiness was for every Christian. Surely the higher, more spiritual, more devoted life is the normal life, and of course it includes doing our duty and saying our prayers. Our task now is to discover something of this Way to which we are called. I write as one who has been influenced by certain traditions and movements within the Church, as will be plainly seen, but I must say at once that to write on such a theme is not the same as to have attained. I am comforted that even John Wesley never claimed to have experienced the perfect love which he taught. I do know that the line of teaching I shall try to unfold has produced its fair share of saints, some of whom it has been my privilege to know.

* This led James Hannay, better known as George A. Birmingham, the writer of novels about Irish life, to a study of the origin of Christian mysticism.

Chapter Two

Some Basic Assumptions

The heart of our religion is a personal experience of God through our Lord Jesus Christ. Such a simple statement, at first sight so clear and self-evident, actually begs a number of questions. Who is this Lord Jesus Christ? Where do we learn of him, and can we be sure that what we learn is trustworthy? What do we mean by a personal experience of God? Is the Christ of experience the same as the Jesus of history? In other words, before we get very far in our discussion of the Call to Holiness, we have to involve ourselves with Christian doctrine. I shall not here attempt even a brief summary of the Christian Faith. But there are certain truths which to me are particularly meaningful, and which underlie all else that I shall say about holiness. If you like, they represent a point of view, a school of thought. I do not apologize for this. One may try hard to appreciate other points of view, but there are always some things which are peculiarly one's own. These are the foundations of one's faith. I find there are six which I want to have firmly laid. Without them the building will be in danger of falling.

1. Since the question of authority in religion is basic to all else, it is well to begin by asserting the supremacy and authority of Holy Scripture. It may be said that this is a truth held by the whole Church. Certainly Article VI of the Anglican Church teaches very clearly that 'Holy Scripture containeth all things necessary to salvation'. In Article VIII

the three Creeds are accepted for this reason : 'for they may be proved by most certain warrants of Scripture'. Indeed every branch of the Church gives a high place to the Bible as the Word of God. It may be no more than a matter of emphasis to say that I want to give it the supreme place, and allow to tradition and to reason only a subservient role. A well-known phrase, much in use in some circles, is : 'The Church to teach and the Bible to prove'. I confess I am not enamoured of this saying. I should prefer to say : 'The Bible to teach, the Church to witness to that teaching, and where necessary to be corrected by it'. I see the Church as always under the judgment of the Word of God, even though it is itself, in the words of Article XX, a witness and a keeper of holy Writ.

It would be wrong to suppose that those who think as I do have no place for tradition. We are aware of the danger of making the Word of God of no affect by our traditions, but there is nevertheless a right kind of tradition, which is the accumulated understanding by the living, ongoing Church, of the truth revealed in the Scriptures. Any Christian who sets himself up to expound the Bible in a sense which is clean contrary to its accepted meaning would be wise to examine his heart for the possible sin of pride. When Charles Simeon refused to be bound by a theological system, and declared himself a slave of the Word, he was not ignoring all that others had taught from the Bible. The point is that the true tradition is what is handed down of wisdom drawn from the Bible, never apart from the Bible, still less contrary to it.

As there is a place for tradition rightly understood, so there is also a place for human reason. It is certainly right to point out that man's mind, along with every other part of his being, is tainted with evil. Yet the Christian mind is renewed by the Holy Spirit and can thus be used to discern God's truth. But again, it is always God's truth as revealed by him, not as discovered unaided by man. Such an attitude to Scripture has sometimes given rise to the charge of fundamentalism. As a matter of fact the term 'Fundamentalism' has a perfectly respectable origin, and as first used meant no more than strict orthodoxy. But as it is commonly used, it is taken to mean a naive and unthinking attitude to the Bible, which is certainly not true of sound scholarship today. For a conservative point of view on the Scriptures we can refer to the series of commentaries issued by the I.V.P. No one can read these works and still believe that such scholars are wedded to an uncritical obscuranticism.

Nevertheless we need be in no doubt that the Bible is uniquely inspired. This belief is not affected by questions of the authorship or the date of a particular book. We know that God speaks through his Word, even though it is sometimes clothed in very earthy form. As with Christ, the living Word, the human and the divine are held together in one complete whole. And it is loyalty to Christ which in the end determines our attitude to Scripture. The Old Testament was our Lord's Bible. Like all Jews, he knew large parts of it by heart, he meditated on it constantly, and used it as a weapon in spiritual conflict. Though he read deeper meanings into it than his contemporaries, it was to him the Word of the Lord just as it stood. More than this, he saw it as the book which pointed to him. So in a double sense the Old Testament is our Lord's own Book. The New Testament is clearly, to the Christian, the completion and fulfilment of the Old. In it Christ speaks, and this is convincing witness to its inspiration. It is worth recalling the testimony of J. B. Phillips when he was translating the Epistles. He says that again and again he felt like an electrician re-wiring an ancient house without being able to 'turn the mains off'.

2. It follows that I find that I am satisfied with the traditional orthodoxy of the Creeds. I have no difficulty in

subcribing to such articles as the Virgin Birth, the Resurrection of Christ as a literal event 'on the third day', or the Second Advent. In this I would claim to hold the Catholic Faith in its fulness, and am unmoved by attempts to make it more palatable to modern man, which in reality whittle away the objective facts of the gospel. I do not feel in the least apologetic about maintaining 'the faith which has been once and for all entrusted to the saints' (Jude 3). Within this body of truth, however, I value a particular evangelical emphasis on the death of Christ and its atoning efficacy. There are those for whom the message of Christianity is centred in the Incarnation. They stress the humanity of Jesus and the significance for us of the affirmation *He was made Man*. Others again find the good news chiefly in the ongoing triumph of the spirit of the living Christ. I unhesitatingly believe that the Cross is central. The words of Mark 10.45, 'For the Son of Man himself did not come to be served but to serve', do not contain the gospel message until they have been completed, 'and to give his life as a ransom for many'. The living Christ is more than a continuing influence. He is the Living One who says : 'I was dead and now I am to live for ever and ever, and I hold the keys of death and of the underworld' (Rev. 1.18).

We may allow that such an evangelical emphasis needs the contribution of other theological outlooks if we are to hold the Faith in proper proportion. This may well be so. Nevertheless I would hold strongly that the Cross of Christ as a 'full, perfect and sufficient sacrifice, oblation and satisfaction for the sins of the whole world' cannot be omitted without emptying the gospel of its meaning. The phrase quoted is from the Book of Common Prayer, and emphasizes that the death of Christ achieved reconciliation between God and man. There are many theories of the Atonement, and they are not necessarily mutually exclusive. But I do not believe we can ever be satisfied with a merely subjective view. Many, perhaps most, evangelicals think of Christ's death as substitutionary, meaning that in some infinitely loving way he took our place and died in our stead. Some hesitate to use a word which is not in the New Testament, and which has sometimes been misinterpreted to suggest views which are both crude and unbiblical. But Scripture itself is overwhelming in its testimony to the objectivity of the Atonement. Certainly the profound words of 2 Cor. 5.21 seem to justify the word substitute : 'For our sake God made the sinless one into sin, so that in him we might become the goodness of God'. If we ask why the Cross is so central to the message we proclaim, the short answer is that it appears to be so in the New Testatment. But it is also because if we take a realistic view of sin, righteousness and judgment, we shall find in Christ crucified the only refuge, the divinely appointed way of reconciliation.

3. A third basic assumption in all that follows is insistence on the new birth as a conscious experience, issuing in new life and changed behaviour. The realistic view of sin mentioned above includes the recognition of the depravity of the human heart. Man's fallen nature is incapable of improvement by education or enlightenment, and needs the infusion of the divine nature by a miracle of grace. This necessity is recognized by all orthodox Christians, though some seem to equate the new birth with baptism *ex opere operato*. The scriptural position seems to me to be that new birth can only be shown to have taken place when there is evidence of spiritual life and moral change. Baptism, whether of those who have already consciously repented and believed the gospel, or of infants who cannot as yet do those things for themselves, is the outward and visible sign. I have sometimes been accused, by those who hold a different view of baptismal regeneration, of confusing the new birth with conversion. To this we might reply :

'What God has joined together, let no man put asunder'. To many who have already received the sacrament we nevertheless need to preach, 'Ye must be born again' (John 3.7. A.V.). The story is told of George Whitefield that, when a lady asked him why he so constantly preached from that text, he replied, 'Madam, because ye must be born again'.

Holy Scripture is emphatic that unless there is a manifestation of the divine life there is no ground for claiming new birth. The First Epistle of John gives some searching tests. Marks of the regenerate man are that he is righteous (2.29), that he does not live a life of sin (3.9), that he loves his fellow-men (4.7), that he acknowledges Jesus as Lord (5.1), and that he conquers the world (5.4). On this last point Bishop Westcott comments : 'It is by the introduction of the spiritual, the eternal, that we obtain a true standard for things, and so can overcome the temptations which spring out of a narrow, earthly, temporal estimate.' No Christian would claim that he reaches the standard set out by John. That would be perfectionism run riot, and the same Epistle repudiates the possibility of sinlessness (1.8). But the new life of the regenerate recognizes the ideal, strives towards it, and is sensitive and penitent in the face of failure. The new heart is habitually humble and contrite, sometimes in circumstances where the unregenerate might find cause for complacency and self-congratulation.

4. Another distinctive truth of great importance, though often misunderstood, is the doctrine of assurance. I have spoken of the new birth as a *conscious* experience. This means that we know it has happened. We ought to rejoice in such words as John 5.24, 'I tell you most solemnly, whoever listens to my words, and believes in the one who sent me, has eternal life; without being brought to judgment he has passed from death to life'. Again in John 10.27, 28, 'The sheep that belong to me listen to my voice; I know them

and they follow me. I give them eternal life; they will never be lost and no one will ever steal them from me'. We can share Paul's confidence when he wrote : 'I know who it is that I have put my trust in, and I have no doubt at all that he is able to take care of all that I have entrusted to him until that Day' (2 Tim. 1.1). Clearly it would be arrogant in the extreme to claim assurance of salvation if that salvation depended in any way on our own worthiness. But as it is by God's grace alone, it is glorifying to God to accept in all humility the assurance he gives. It is, by the same token, dishonouring to him to doubt his forgiveness, his acceptance of us just as we are for Christ's sake, his gift of eternal life.

Not that assurance rests on isolated texts of Scripture such as those already quoted. Rather is it grounded in the character of God as revealed in Christ and witnessed to in the whole Bible. In particular the message of the Cross as a full atonement for sin brings the certainty of God's pardon. This is why evangelicals, with others, have always greatly valued the Lord's Supper. For here the benefits of Christ's passion are set forth and received by faith. Similarly the other gospel sacrament of Baptism is accepted as the pledge of Christ's power to save. When Martin Luther was tempted to doubt his position before God he would solemnly affirm : '*Baptizatus sum*'. God's grace pledged to him in the sacrament was greater than his doubts or fears, his feelings or his failings. Always we should try to turn the thoughts of the doubter away from himself to the unchangeable facts of the gospel and the living Christ himself.

In doing this the individual verse or promise of Scripture is not to be neglected. Provided words are not wrenched from their context to give them a meaning never intended, there is much value in this use. We have an example of such texts in the Comfortable Words of the Anglican Liturgy. Some words much loved by evangelical preachers,

Revelation 3.20, are another good illustration. Here the risen and glorified Christ is depicted as standing at the door of the lukewarm Church of Laodicea and knocking. His appeal is to any individual who will respond : 'If one of you hears me calling and opens the door, I will come in to share his meal, side by side with him'. The application of these words to Christ seeking admission to the human heart is entirely appropriate, and, as a simple statement of fact, the words 'I will come in' have been accepted as a promise of his coming into the life by hundreds who date the beginning of their Christian experience from such a moment. This is but a single illustration of the use of a Bible text. There are many others. But again it needs to be emphasized that assurance rests on the whole of what God is, and has done, and has said, and not on any one small bit of truth.

Always it is the Holy Spirit who applies the word and truth of God to the heart. John Wesley laid great stress on what he called 'the inward witness', a reference to Romans 8.15 : 'The Spirit himself and our spirit bear united witness that we are children of God'. Wesley would be the first to stress that this inner conviction, brought by the Holy Spirit, is dependent upon the solid teaching of the Word of God. It is not merely a religious feeling, a frame of mind. Such can be dangerously misleading, and as a basis for assurance can only lead to doubt and despair. Our forefathers in the last century warned against trusting in 'frames', and none has put it more clearly than Edward Mote in these words :

> My hope is built on nothing less
> Than Jesus' blood and righteousness;
> I dare not trust the sweetest frame,
> But wholly lean on Jesus' name.
>> On Christ, the solid Rock, I stand;
>> All other ground is sinking sand.

23

Nevertheless there is such a thing as the inward witness, a firm conviction, implanted by the Spirit, which is not in the least dependent on the ups and downs of religious feeling.

5. The priesthood of all believers. The once-and-for-all nature of the sacrifice of Christ is a precious part of the gospel. We see him as the perfect fulfilment of Old Testament priesthood and sacrifice, and note that the Greek word meaning priest is used in the New Testament only of the Jewish priest, of our Lord himself, and of the whole body of the Church, the holy and royal priesthood mentioned in 1 Peter 2.5, 9. It is never applied to a Christian minister, who is referred to rather as a presbyter. Evangelicals have made much of this because they have seen the danger of exalting a human priest to the position of mediator which can be filled by Christ alone. The teaching of the Epistle to the Hebrews on the uniqueness of Christ's priesthood and the completeness of the offering of himself once made has seemed to need safeguarding. No doubt there has been misunderstanding on both sides of the catholic-protestant confrontation, and controversy has now given place to dialogue. And in any case it ought to be stated that the stand against what were regarded as false views of priesthood was primarily a positive witness for the gospel, not a negative protest.

What we need to see clearly is that the entire body of Christians is a priesthood. All whom our Lord has freed from their sins by his blood, he had made a kingdom of priests to his God and Father. (See Revelation 1.5, 6. R.S.V.) Not that there can ever be any other high priest than our Lord, or any sacrifice but Calvary. But the redeemed company is a 'holy priesthood that offers the spiritual sacrifices which Jesus Christ has made acceptable to God' (1 Pet. 2.5). Like Israel of old, they are '*a chosen race, a royal priesthood, a consecrated nation, a people set apart* to sing the praises of God' (1 Pet. 2.9). Just as Israel was called to be a blessing to all nations of the world in the promise made to Abraham, which promise was fulfilled in the coming of Christ, so the Church is to stand on the Godward side of the world. The whole Christian fellowship offers its sacrifice of praise and intercession, and mediates the Word of God to the world through its witness.

An understanding of this truth gives rise to certain characteristics in the life of holiness to which we must return in detail, so our mention of them here is only a passing reference. One is the place given to intercession as an activity of every Christian, one evidence of which is the emphasis on the prayer meeting. A second is recognition of the obligation to witness for Christ, not only to one's friends and neighbours, but to all, of every religion and of none, in the whole world. And a third is the prominence given to the laity in all this. One of the greatest agencies for the spread of the gospel has been the Church Missionary Society, founded in 1799 as a direct outcome of the evangelical revival. It is not without significance that it has always maintained that it is a lay society, and that its policy has been governed from its earliest days by the determination to 'put prayer first'.

6. Sanctification by the Holy Spirit. We have already mentioned the evangelical emphasis on the new birth as a work of the Holy Spirit in the heart of the believer. We have seen that assurance of salvation is brought by the witness of the Spirit. Much remains to be said about the Holy Spirit, and in a study of the call to holiness this will be a major preoccupation. In the course of our investigation we shall find no unanimity about the exact manner in which the work of sanctification is accomplished. Scripture is very rich in its allusions to the subject. Phrases like 'sanctify you wholly', 'perfect love', 'baptized with the Holy Spirit',

'filled with the Spirit', to mention but a few, have been understood by different people in different ways. At various times in history discussion has been centred on one or other aspect of the truth, and equally godly people have ranged themselves on one side or the other. Today the division is probably chiefly between those who stress the charismatic gifts of the Spirit and those who do not. Even there the division is not clearly defined.

All Christians however, without exception, believe that it is the Holy Spirit alone who enables us to live a holy life. A well-known hymn contains lines which all would endorse –

> And every virtue we possess,
> And every victory won,
> And every thought of holiness,
> Are his alone.

Although this seems to make sanctification a very personal and individual matter, as indeed it is, we must also recognize the work of the Spirit in creating fellowship. Within the local group of those who share in the communion of the Holy Spirit there is the increase of love, joy, peace, and all the other elements which together are the fruit of the Spirit. It was John Wesley who said that there is no such thing as a solitary Christian. We need have no difficulty in accepting the statement of the Church of England Catechism : 'I believe in God the Holy Ghost, who sanctifieth me, *and all the elect people of God*'. We would indeed go further and say that it is only within that fellowship that individual holiness can flourish. We are, in the words of the R.S.V. of 1 Corinthians 1.2, 'called to be saints together'.

Chapter Three

Holiness: What Is It?

To answer the question which is the title of this chapter would require a book in itself. Yet some kind of definition is required if we are to understand the tradition of sanctity I am trying to expound. What do we really mean by holiness? We have seen that all agree that ultimately sanctification is the work of the Holy Spirit, but what *is* sanctification, sanctity, holiness? Bishop Stephen Neill opens his book *Christian Holiness* with the same dilemma. He says :

'We all profess to believe one *holy*, catholic and apostolic Church. We know that the Church is called to be holy, and that the individual members of the Church also ought to be holy. But the moment that we attempt to put content in familiar phrases we begin to run into difficulties.'

We must begin with the holiness of God. The vision which Isaiah had in the Temple* was of the Lord 'high and lifted up'. The heavenly beings covered their faces in his presence, and cried 'Holy, holy, holy is the Lord of hosts'. The effect on Isaiah was to make him feel his wretched state, his lost condition, his uncleanness. The majesty, the transcendence, of God seems to be the root idea of his holiness. He is utterly above and beyond all other 'gods'. 'Who among the gods is your like, Yahweh? Who is your like, *majestic in holiness*?' (Ex. 15.11). He is completely different from man. 'For I am God, not man : I am the Holy One

* See Isaiah 6.1–8.

in your midst' (Hos. 11.9). When God's character is fully revealed in Jesus Christ it is still the same. He is the 'only Sovereign, the King of kings and Lord of lords, who alone has immortality and dwells in unapproachable light, whom no man has ever seen or can see' (1 Tim. 6.15, 16. R.S.V.). This 'otherness' of God is basic to the idea of holiness. If a single word is demanded to describe it, that word must be 'separation'. God's holiness sets him apart from all else.

Yet the separateness of God in his holiness does not hinder his closeness to man in his grace. The Holy One is 'in your midst'. Jesus our great High Priest is described in Hebrews 7.26 as 'holy, innocent and uncontaminated, beyond the influence of sinners (separated from sinners – R.S.V.), and raised up above the heavens'. Yet this is the same Jesus who was known as the friend of sinners. It was precisely because he was holy that he could give himself unreservedly in friendship to sinners, making himself one with them in redeeming love, yet remaining always uncontaminated. God's holiness is certainly a mark of his transcendence, but it also has a deeply moral significance. In the words of Habakkuk 1.13, 'Your eyes are too pure to rest on wickedness'. Professor R. A. Finlayson puts it : 'Holiness is a term for the moral excellence of God and his freedom from all limitation in his moral perfection. In this exalted sense God only is holy and so the standard of ethical purity in his creatures'.* Thus the two ideas, of separateness and moral perfection, are united in the holiness of God.

In the Old Testament the word holy is used often of times, places, buildings, furnishings, garments, and of persons connected with the worship of God. The Sabbath is a holy day (Ex. 16.23). The place where Moses stood at the burning bush was holy ground (Ex. 3.5). A part of the tabernacle, and later of the temple, was designated the holy place

* *The New Bible Dictionary*, Article 'Holiness, Holy, Saints'. **I.V.P.**

(Lev. 16.2 and many other references). The ark was holy (2 Chron. 35.3), as were the priestly robes (Ex. 28.2). All these and many other things were holy because they were separated from common use and set apart entirely for God's glory. But the note of moral perfection was not absent, for everything had to be made according to the pattern revealed by the Lord to Moses on the mountain (see Ex. 25.40). Meticulous care of the minutiae of worship gave to the people a deep sense of reverence.

There was, however, a danger in undue importance being attached to outward detail at the expense of the inward spirit. The prophets thundered against religion which failed to produce ethical change. Feasts and festivals were a part of normal worship, but Amos represents God as saying : 'I hate and despise your feasts, I take no pleasure in your solemn festivals' (Amos 5.21). Oblations and music, if not accompanied by penitence, were unacceptable to God, 'But let justice flow like water and integrity like an unfailing stream'. In Jeremiah's day too there was worship without amendment of life, calling forth the stern rebuke : 'Put no trust in delusive words like these : This is the sanctuary of Yahweh, the sanctuary of Yahweh, the sanctuary of Yahweh ! But if you do amend your behaviour and your actions . . . then here in this place I will stay with you, in the land that long ago I gave to your fathers for ever' (Jer. 7.4–7).

This latter passage introduces us to two special elements in the Old Testament : the holy land and the holy people. For the Hebrews the land was a God-given inheritance, and to desert it was in some sense to desert him. Worship was to be offered in the appointed place. Whatever may have been the rights and wrongs of this at various stages in the history of Israel, our Lord gave the death blow to it for the new age which began with his coming. To the Samaritan woman who raised the question of the correct place to offer worship he said : 'Believe me, woman, the hour is coming when you will worship the Father neither on this mountain nor in Jerusalem. . . . God is spirit, and those who worship must worship in spirit and truth' (John 4.21–24.) In a few words Jesus demolished the idea of any one place being holier than another. We may certainly speak today of the Holy Land because of its associations with the People of God and our Lord himself. But any idea that God is more real in Bethlehem than he is in Birmingham or Boston is wholly foreign to the Christian gospel. And the same goes for Rome, or Canterbury, or Keswick.

In order to make the point I have perhaps over-emphasized it. No one objects to the setting apart of buildings for worship, or to the association of the Keswick Convention with a natural beauty spot. No one need be ashamed of a sense of awe when kneeling in a place where worship has been offered for a thousand years, or of a quickened devotion when standing by the Lake of Galilee. But no place on earth can ever be *the* holy place. Jacob's experience at Bethel can be repeated anywhere that God chooses to reveal himself, and the two or three gathered in the Saviour's name will find his presence whether they meet in a cathedral or a barn. It is Christ's presence with them which constitutes them *the holy people*.

This expression was used originally of Israel. 'Now therefore, if you will obey my voice and keep my covenant, you shall be my own possession among all peoples; for all the earth is mine, and you shall be to me a kingdom of priests and a holy nation' (Ex. 19.5, 6. R.S.V.). The Jerusalem Bible renders those last words 'a consecrated nation'. By God's sovereign will Israel had been chosen to be the special People through which he would eventually reveal himself to the whole world. Christians see the promise made to Abraham, that 'all the tribes of the earth shall bless themselves by you', fulfilled in Christ who is a light to lighten the Gentiles as well as the glory of his People Israel. Without surrendering our belief in the purpose of God for those whom he first called to be his People (e.g. Rom. 11.11–29), we can see clearly that the concept of the holy people is transferred in the New Testament to the Christian Church. The words of 1 Peter 2.9, 10, are clearly addressed to Christian believers : 'But you are a chosen race, a royal priesthood, a consecrated nation, a people set apart to sing the praises of God who called you out of darkness into his wonderful light. Once you were not a people at all and now you are the People of God; once you were outside the mercy and now you have been given mercy'.

This 'holy people' is what we speak of in the Creed as the One Holy, Catholic and Apostolic Church. It is when we come to interpreting the meaning of the clause that divergence between the catholic and the evangelical appears. Broadly speaking the catholic sees the Church as a divinely constituted institution in which the Faith is safe-guarded by an unbroken succession of bishops from the Apostles to the present time. It is this institution which is holy, and within it men may grow in holiness. This brief summary is much too general to be wholly fair, and it certainly contains elements which the evangelical would not deny (for example that we grow in holiness within the fellowship of the Church). To the evangelical the Church is catholic because it is universal, and apostolic because it holds the truths taught by the Apostles as recorded in Scripture. And it is holy because it is made up of those who are united to Christ and living holy lives. Again the summary is too general to be anything like adequate.

Probably the best way of arriving at this evangelical conception of the holiness of the Church is by a study of the commonest New Testament name given to Christians, namely 'the saints'. That it refers simply to ordinary Christians, and not to a few outstandingly holy people, is clear from its use in the Acts and the Epistles on numerous occasions. Paul's Epistle to the Philippians, for instance, is addressed to 'all the saints in Christ Jesus' (Phil. 1.1); the same letter ends with his greeting 'to every one of the saints in Christ Jesus' (Phil. 4.21) and adds: 'All the saints send their greetings, especially those of the imperial household' (Phil. 4.22). The interesting thing is that although the word is used in the New Testament over sixty times it never once occurs in the singular. A Christian, it would seem, is to be thought of not so much as *a* saint, but as *one* of *the* saints. Yet 'the saints' is a plural, or collective, expression rather than a corporate one. There are other terms, like 'the body of Christ' with its many and varied members, which are corporate. But the saints are a collective group made up of individuals. They are holy as a group because they are holy as individuals, and not *vice versa*. If we consider the other great word used by Chritian believers, namely 'brethren', we find that it also is collective rather than corporate. The relationship, both of one believer to another and of each to God, is personal and individual. Without neglecting the 'body' metaphor, we must give full weight to the emphasis in the New Testament on the Church as made up of saints. The Church is as holy as its members.

What then is the holiness of the saints? It is worth noting that the Greek noun translated 'saints' is exactly the same as the adjective 'holy'. 'Saints' and 'holy ones' are one and the same. And their holiness consists, like the holiness of God, in their being separated, set apart for a special purpose. The New English Bible uses the expression 'His dedicated people' (Rom. 1.7) which conveys the meaning, provided we remember that it is God, and not the believer himself, who does the dedicating. Christians are set apart *by* God, and *for* God. In Christ we belong to God absolutely. Sanctification is the working out of this 'belonging' in every area of life.

For this reason holiness also has the meaning, as with God himself, of moral excellence. For the Christian believer this means standards of behaviour which accord with the laws, and the revealed will, of God. Consecration must issue in obedience. And whereas the separation aspect of holiness is something known only in the inner recesses of the spirit, the life of consistent well-doing which should result from it is seen and known by all men. It is by integrity and right behaviour that Christians are judged by the world. Hence holiness is seen, and rightly seen, as conformity to the standards shown in the life of Jesus. It is when men see our good works that they will give the praise to our Father in heaven. To this important aspect of our subject we must now turn.

Chapter Four

Holiness: How Does It Show?

It has often been pointed out that the New Testamen
Epistles, those living letters which reflect what the Early
Church believed and taught, can for the most part be divided
into two sections, the doctrinal and the practical. Moreove
there is a close connection between the two. Right behaviou
is the outcome of right belief, and a faith which does no
issue in good works is no faith at all. Holiness is not primarily
a mystical experience but a sound character. Soundnes
suggests health, and there is more than a merely verbal con
nection between holiness and wholeness. There may be
room in the Christian character for vivid experiences of
ecstatic joy, but the hallmark is something more down-to
earth. New Testament holiness is intensely practical
Handley Moule's life of Charles Simeon bears the sub-title
The Biography of a Sane Saint. Perhaps sanity and sanctity
are not always connected in people's minds, but the more we
study the evidence the clearer it becomes that maturity and
balance are key words of Christian holiness. In particula
there needs to be a delicately balanced combination of the
negative aspect of holiness as avoidance of sin and the posi
tive aspect of the practice of goodness.

There must be no shrinking from the negative side. Some
times in our zeal for positive affirmation of Christian virtue
we have lost sight of the fact that there are things to be
renounced : in the words of the Church of England Cate
chism they are 'the devil and all his works, the pomps and

vanity of this wicked world, and all the sinful lusts of the flesh'. Biblical ground for the need to avoid such things is plentiful, and from a number of possible passages to quote I choose Galatians 5.19–21, partly because it is followed immediately by one of the most positive statements of the nature of a holy life. We must not go straight to the fruit of the Spirit without considering first the works of the flesh. 'When self-indulgence is at work the results are obvious : fornication, gross indecency and sexual irresponsibility; idolatry and sorcery; feuds and wrangling, jealousy, bad temper and quarrels; disagreements, factions, envy; drunkenness, orgies and similar things.' It is a fearsome list, but not very different from that in which our Lord himself tells of the things that proceed out of the heart of man (Mark 7.21).

It is often suggested nowadays that Christians are preoccupied with sins of sex. No one who takes the Bible seriously can imagine that the God-given instinct of sex is anything but good in itself. The Song of Solomon, for instance, is unashamedly a human love-poem, and only secondarily an allegory of the love of Christ and his Bride, the Church. But the very sanctity of sexuality makes its abuse the more evil. And although sexual sin is listed first in the passage I have quoted, this is not to say that other sins of wrong relationship with others, or lack of control of oneself, are any less to be avoided. Our Lord's catalogue seems to string together the evil intentions in the heart of man without any suggestion of an order of seriousness : fornication, theft, murder, adultery, avarice, deceit, indecency, envy, slander, pride, folly. All these manifestations of the human heart, that heart which Jeremiah describes as more devious than any other thing, are expressions of self in one form or another, and the condition of following Christ is a willingness to deny, to renounce, to say 'No' to self (Matt. 16.24). The positive step of following Christ involves

35

taking up the cross, which to those who first heard the words could only mean the absolute crucifixion of the self-life.

In the past there has often been encouraged a ruthlessness in dealing with possible sources of temptation which to some has seemed excessively puritanical. To anyone brought up in this tradition the list of those things which a Christian was supposed not to do is well known. It includes dancing, theatre-going, card-playing, to name but a few. One can see the point. Certain forms of dancing could lead to sin. Some stage shows – or films for that matter – can be suggestive in the extreme. Many people associate cards with gambling. Jesus taught that if eye or hand were a cause of sin they should be thrown away rather than that the whole body be cast into hell. What most people today see is that there can be a more discerning and positive attitude to those things which used to be labelled 'worldly'. And what certainly needs to be affirmed is that it is possible to give up all the things which were traditionally taboo and still remain lustful or avaricious in heart. The argument that worldly pleasures take time and energy which might be given to higher things is not convincing; the same can be said of sport, or any other form of innocent recreation. Nor is worldliness confined to pleasures. Jesus spoke of the worries of this world and the lure of riches (Matt. 13.22).

It may be questioned whether the reaction from the earlier view has not gone too far. First-century Christians were bidden : 'You must not love this passing world, or anything that is in the world', and some of the dangers were enumerated : 'the sensual body, the lustful eye, pride in possessions' (1 John 2.15, 16). We shall have reason to return to the subject of the other-worldliness of Christian holiness. Here let me say that the Christian is likened to a soldier on service and an athlete in training : 'In the army, no soldier gets himself mixed up in civilian life, because he must be

at the disposal of the man who enlisted him' (2 Tim. 2.4).
One of Paul's arguments for avoiding things which may be
innocent in themselves, but which are potentially dangerous,
is the effect our behaviour may have on others. His particular concern is with the eating of meat which has been
sacrificed to idols, a matter which is of little interest in our
situation. But the principle holds good. If my indulgence
in a legitimate activity is going to put temptation in the path
of a weaker brother then for his sake I must abstain. To
give one example, a Christian may decide to be teetotal, as
many have in the past and some do still. It may not be
possible to defend this attitude from Scripture in view of
such instances as our Lord's miracle of turning water into
wine. But in our present situation, when alcoholism is a major
threat to society, the total abstainer cannot be said to be
acting irresponsibly.

Having touched on somewhat controversial, and to some
minds trivial, matters, we may be asked the question : Just
how negative can you get? But the point has to be made that
there can be no running away from the negative side of
holiness. The Ten Commandments are in the form of
prohibitions. Our Lord did not destroy the Law, he fulfilled
it. He did not put the positive command to love God and our
neighbour over against the Ten Commandments, as if they
were contradictory. The rule of love was itself already there
in the Old Testament : Jesus strengthened it, and said it
was the key to the Law and the Prophets. But he was careful
also to endorse the prohibitions of the Decalogue, reading
into them a deeper meaning. Thus the command not to kill
becomes a warning of the danger of attitudes to our brother
man which would, if allowed to persist unchanged, lead
to murder. The command not to commit adultery is seen to
include the desires and intentions of the heart. These are
prohibitions. It is not difficult to see how easily we break
every one of the Ten Commandments *in spirit*, even if we

can say with the rich young ruler : 'Master, I have kept all these from my earliest days' (Mark 10.20).

Nevertheless in the New Testament, and not least in our Lord's teaching, we find the greatest emphasis to be on the positive side of holiness. To return to the passage in Galatians, we see the exact opposite of what happens 'when self-indulgence is at work'. 'What the spirit brings is very different : love, joy, peace, patience, kindness, goodness, truthfulness, gentleness and self-control' (Gal. 5.22). This is the fruit, or harvest, of the Spirit. The words are simple, and self-explanatory. Love is put in the first place. In another passage, 2 Peter 1.5–7, love comes last, as the climax : 'Adding goodness to the faith that you have, understanding to your goodness, self-control to your understanding, patience to your self-control, true devotion to your patience, kindness towards your fellow men to your devotion, and, to this kindness, love'. The love here given as the crown of all virtues is the love of complete devotion to the highest good of others. It is the same love of which Paul wrote in 1 Corinthians 13. Henry Drummond's celebrated address on that chapter is entitled *The Greatest Thing in the World*, and that is what love is.

Sometimes 1 Corinthians 13 is referred to as a hymn of love, as if it were primarily a piece of lyrical writing. It certainly has poetic elements, particularly in its opening verses. But the central portion, which describes what love is and does, is a down-to-earth account of holiness. Here devotion is anchored in real situations. To read these words is to be humbled : such a life has been lived only by our Lord, who walked in perfect obedience to the Father. 'Love is very patient, very kind. Love knows no jealousy; love makes no parade, gives itself no airs, is never rude, never selfish, never irritated, never resentful; love is never glad when others go wrong, love is gladdened by goodness, always slow to expose, always eager to believe the best, always hopeful, always patient. Love never disappears' (1 Cor. 13.4–8, Moffatt). If we substitute the name of Jesus for the word love in this passage we get a perfect picture of our Lord's character. Holiness is likeness to Christ, not only in his victory over temptation to sin, but also in his positive life of perfect love, the epitome of all other virtues.

We saw in the last chapter that holiness in the sense of right behaviour is the outcome of that complete consecration to God which is the primary meaning of the word. Thus Paul writes to the Romans : 'Think of God's mercy, my brothers, and worship him, I beg you, in a way that is worthy of thinking beings, by offering your living bodies as a holy sacrifice, truly pleasing to God. Do not model yourselves on the behaviour of the world around you, but let your behaviour change, modelled by your new mind' (Rom. 12.1, 2). The offering of ourselves in full and glad surrender is a recognition of the fact that we do not belong to ourselves. Paul's words to the Corinthians are of wider application than the immediate context, which refers to sexual purity : 'You are not your own property; you have been bought and paid for' (1 Cor. 6.20). The crux of the matter is the surrender of the will, but it has to be remembered that this must be worked out in the very practical details of daily living. No clearer statement of what is involved can be found that Frances Ridley Havergal's hymn which begins

> Take my life, and let it be
> Consecrated, Lord, to Thee.

This general petition is not enough. The consecration of time, talents, speech, possessions, intellect, will and heart all must follow. Every part of our being is his, not ours, and all is held by us in stewardship, not in possession.

Stewardship is a mark of true holiness. It is a pity that the word has come to be used so largely in connection with the use of money, and that 'stewardship campaigns' have on the whole tended to encourage this idea. Stewardship in the New Testament begins with the fact that all that we have, and all that we are, belongs to God. We are his by creation, and we are his by redemption. Consequently – to concentrate for the moment on that one aspect of the subject – our money belongs to him. A large proportion of our money is needed to keep us, and those dependent on us, in reasonable efficiency, but in recognition that all that we have is held in stewardship we set apart a proportion to be given back to God for his work. In the Old Testament the People of God were required by the Law to give one-tenth of all they possessed, and it has been characteristic of much Bible-based teaching to make this a minimum for Christian giving. Yet how important it is to remember that, when the tithe is paid, the remaining nine-tenths still belongs to God and not to ourselves. So we shall expect to find – and a fairly long experience in pastoral work leads me to believe that we do find – that among those who are careful about tithing there is also a responsible attitude towards all money matters. The result is wise spending, modest standards of living, and an abhorrence of debts.

I have chosen to illustrate the principal of stewardship by the use of money because it is a very concrete thing which concerns us all. But all our material possessions are equally subject to the same spiritual laws. The home, the garden, the car are all at God's disposal. So also is that most precious commodity, our time. Here, as in tithing, a proportion can be set apart as specially devoted to God. The weekly day of rest and worship and the daily devotional period for prayer and Bible reading are obvious examples, and all Christians have always emphasized their importance. But the setting apart of one day in seven is not an end in itself : it is a means of ensuring that all our days are rightly used in the service of God. 'Six days shalt thou labour' is a part of the

4th Commandment, and no one can deny that strict observance of the Lord's Day has usually gone hand in hand with diligence in work and a horror of time-wasting on weekdays. Similarly the talents that God has given to all of us in varying quantities are to be developed and used in his service, and for his glory.

If stewardship teaches us that all our life belongs to God, it is clearly a mistake to draw too hard and fast a line between the sacred and the secular. Most Christians are not on the whole drawn to the kind of monastic ideals which have motivated the religious orders, not, let it be hoped, from a reluctance to face the difficulties of the 'religious' life, but from fear of encouraging a dual standard. Holiness is to be lived in the world, not apart from it. In so far as some degree of withdrawal from the world is necessary in order to maintain a close walk with God, this is something for every Christian, not just a spiritual élite. Life is not only religion, any more than religion is to be regarded as merely one department of life. Work, recreation, social relationships, are all a part of the life which is to be sanctified. Christ is to be glorified in our career, undertaken by his guidance, and worked at with all our natural ability and vigour, as well as with divine help. This is true whether the career be that of a missionary or a merchant, a parson or a postman. The initials frequently put in old days on the fly leaf of a book, or in a wall of a building, A.M.D.G. (ad majorem dei gloriam) should be mentally placed over every occupation of the Christian, be it business, pleasure, or social or family duty.

Illustrations of the attractiveness of consistent Christian living could be drawn from many different ages, backgrounds and countries. On the whole most Christians have placed the greatest emphasis on home and family life as well as personal discipline. One thinks of the group of prominent laymen known as the Clapham Sect, of whom William Wilberforce was the best known. In a way they were not typical, for they came from the wealthy classes and were among the rulers of the nation. This, however, only accentuates the kind of lives they lived. Temptations to self-indulgence were many and strong. But these men kept strict watch on their time each day. Wilberforce's time-table, found after his death, revealed not only so many hours for prayer, study, business and rest, but a column in which to record the amount of time squandered. It was the same with their money. Henry Thornton before he married gave away six-sevenths of his income, and afterwards one-third. Wilberforce is remembered chiefly for his work to abolish the slave trade, and it involved twenty years of labour which would have daunted a lesser man. But behind this public image was a humble man of God, devoted to home and family, gracious and amusing in conversation. True sanctity is not tense and unnatural, but relaxed and human. In a word, it is Christ-like.

Chapter Five

Motives for Holy Living

Motives are notoriously difficult to assess. Can I be quite sure that even the most altruistic act I have ever done was not motivated, at least in part, by self in one of its many forms? We can think at once of reasons why we might want to be holy of which, when they are brought to light, we must be ashamed. The most obvious is the desire to be thought well of by others, to gain a reputation, even a reputation for being humble! Or there is the wish to be on good terms with oneself, to be able to hold one's head high and walk with a confident step, to 'feel good'. It is but a short step from this to feeling better than others. Again there is the search for happines as an end in itself, happiness which Christians have always taught is inseparable from holy living. Once again there is the desire to conform to the standard of a particular group to which we belong. All such motives, when analysed, will be found to be selfish, and act as incentives, not to holiness, but to formalism or even to downright hypocrisy.

We have already suggested that motives may be mixed. Some of the strongest incentives to a life of true holiness may be seen to contain the possibility of corruption and falsity. Every part of man's being is infected with evil and we need not be surprised if we find, on searching our hearts, that our motives are not one hundred per cent pure. Indeed there comes a time when we should cease to probe the dark recesses of our corrupt nature, and cast ourselves on the mercy of our all-seeing, all-knowing, and yet all-loving Father. He is the God 'unto whom all hearts are open, all desires known, and from whom no secrets are hid'. And when we continue in that same Collect to ask God to 'cleanse the thoughts of our hearts by the inspiration of thy Holy Spirit' there is no part of us more in need of cleansing than our motives. We need to pray –

> Search all my thoughts, the secret springs,
> The motives that control.

But having prayed for sincerity in this way it is well to heed the eminently sound advice : 'For every look at self, take ten looks at Christ'. We do not need to tear ourselves apart in searching for wrong motives for seeking holiness.

To turn now to right and true incentives, even though they are capable of being debased, surely one is the desire to live a life consistent with our Christian profession. One of the elementary truths of the gospel is that we are required to confess Christ openly. An avowal of faith is linked with belief in Christ's resurrection in what may well have been an early requirement for baptism. 'If your lips confess that Jesus is Lord and if you believe in your heart that God raised him from the dead, then you will be saved' (Rom. 10.9). Jesus himself said something similar : 'So if anyone declares himself for me in the presence of men, I will declare myself for him in the presence of my Father in heaven' (Matt. 10.32). It is unthinkable that a Christian should not declare himself. But when he does, he is at the same time committing himself to a life consistent with his words. All of us fear, and rightly so, that what we are will belie what we say. Certainly the motive at times may be mixed with a wrong fear of losing face by our inconsistency, the dread of being called a hypocrite. But the desire to back up our spoken witness with a life that is worthy of the gospel is a wholly right instinct. Consistent living is like a light shining in the sight of men, that 'seeing your good works they may give the praise to your Father in heaven' (Matt. 5.16). The converse is also true : inconsistent behaviour not only contradicts the spoken profession, but also dishonours God. These words of Paul hold a solemn truth : 'By boasting about the Law and then disobeying it, you bring God into contempt. As scripture says : *It is your fault that the name of God is blasphemed among the pagans'* (Rom. 2.23, 24).

A second motive for holiness is the will to live with a good conscience. I have spoken already of the wrong motive of wanting to 'feel good'. There is a subtle difference between this selfish purpose and the desire 'to keep a clear conscience at all times before God and man' (Acts 24.16). Conscience is by no means an infallible guide, and people throughout history have done, and still do, surprising things in the name of conscience. But the Christian conscience can be educated by the Holy Spirit to become sensitive to the will of God as expressed in his Word. Mistakes may still be made. Christian people will be found acting conscientiously on both sides of such moral issues as pacifism or the indissolubility of marriage. But the New Testament makes it clear that a good conscience is a powerful weapon in our spiritual armour. Thus Timothy is urged to 'fight like a good soldier with faith and a good conscience for your weapons'. And the passages goes on : 'Some people have put conscience aside and wrecked their faith in consequence' (1 Tim. 1.19).

Faith and a good conscience go hand in hand. If our faith is justified before others by consistent living, it is justified to ourselves by a clear conscience. It is certain that conscience cannot be clear unless we 'strive for peace with all men, and for the holiness without which no one will see the Lord' (Heb. 12.14, R.S.V.). There is a sense in which a quiet conscience, evidence of the pursuit of holiness (though not of absolute perfection), is a part of our assurance of salvation. We have already looked at the passage in 2 Peter 1 which bids us supplement faith with goodness, goodness with understanding, understanding with self-control, self-control with patience, patience with true devotion, devotion with kindness, and kindness with love, a wonderful picture of progress in holiness. The passage goes on (N.E.B.) : 'These are gifts which, if you possess and foster them, will keep you from being either useless or barren in the knowledge of our Lord Jesus Christ. The man who lacks them is short-sighted and blind; he has forgotten how he was cleansed from his former sins. *All the more then, my friends, exert yourselves to clinch God's choice and calling of you. If you behave so, you will never come to grief*'. Here then is a powerful incentive to holiness. In the words of the Authorized Version, 'Give diligence to make your calling and election sure'.

If the first motive we have considered concerns our life as witness to others, and the second our life with our own conscience, the third is to do with our life before God. It is a simple matter of fact that a holy God requires his people to be holy. 'You therefore must be holy because I am holy' (Lev. 11.45) is written large across the pages of the Old Testament. What has been called the greatest saying in the Old Testament begins with the words : 'He has showed you, O man, what is good; and what does the Lord require of you . . . ?' (Mal. 6.8). We need to recover the sense of a God who makes demands, and those demands are for likeness to himself. In the saying just quoted it is 'to do justice, to love kindness, and to walk humbly with your God'. The New Testament requirements, as we saw in the last chapter, are certainly not less demanding than the Old. Our Lord's summing up of the commands of God is quite uncompromising : 'You must therefore be perfect just as your heavenly Father is perfect' (Matt. 5.48).

It is possible to present the requirements of God in such a way as to suggest that only when the demands are met can we be in right relationship with him. This is quite contrary to the gospel. In actual fact no one has ever completely and absolutely done justice, loved kindness, and walked humbly with God. No one has ever been perfect as the heavenly Father is perfect. No one, that is to say, except Christ. The absolute demands of God, revealed even more fully in Christ himself than in the Old Testament Law, are to drive us into the arms of that same Christ, our only Saviour. Toplady has expressed this in words which have only lost their power because we have become so accustomed to them :

> Not the labours of my hands
> Can fulfil thy Law's demands;
> Could my zeal no respite know,
> Could my tears for ever flow,
> All for sin could not atone,
> Thou must save and thou alone.

The demands of God upon us remain after we have fled for refuge to the Rock of Ages. We cannot escape from the fact that God wants us to be holy as he himself is holy. But there is a new motive to be introduced.

It is the motive of gratitude for the grace of God freely bestowed in Christ. If holiness were the means by which we were brought into right relationship with God, no one would be saved, for none is holy enough to qualify. That is why Rock of Ages, which could well be a prayer of contrition for the greatest sinner in the world, was actually entitled by its author 'A living and dying prayer for the holiest believer in the world'. No one is ever beyond the need for God's saving grace. No one is ever acceptable for what he is in himself, but only accepted in Christ. As Paul wrote in Ephesians 1, we are chosen in Christ, destined in love to be God's children through Jesus Christ, accepted in the Beloved. In him we have redemption through his blood, the forgiveness of sins according to the riches of his grace which he lavished on us. In him we have a part in his eternal purpose; we are sealed with the promised Holy Spirit, which is the guarantee of our eternal inheritance. All this is free, given bountifully by our loving God to us who deserve nothing but his righteous anger. We were, as Paul goes on in Ephesians 2 to say, dead through the trespasses and sins in which we once walked. But God, who is rich in mercy, out of the great love with which he loved us, has made us alive together with Christ. What higher motive for holy living can there be than to live to the praise of his glorious grace?

> Ransomed, healed, restored, forgiven,
> Who like me his praise should sing?

In point of fact this overwhelming gratitude for what God in Christ has done for us is far and away the strongest motive for holy living. 'The love of Christ', says Paul, 'overwhelms us when we reflect that if one man has died for all, then all men should be dead; and the reason he died for all was so that living men should live no longer for themselves, but for him who died and was raised to life for them' (2 Cor. 5.14, 15). If we remember that showing forth praise to God is not only with our lips but in our lives, we have a wonderful expression of this motive for holiness in C. A. Alington's hymn, based on 1 Peter 2.9 –

48

Tell the praise of him who called you
Out of darkness into light,
Broke the fetters that enthralled you,
Gave you freedom, peace and sight :
Tell the tale of sins forgiven,
Strength renewed and hope restored,
Till the earth, in tune with heaven,
Praise and magnify the Lord.

Rather less accomplished as verse, but none the less pro-
foundly true theologically, and in experience, are these
simple lines :

I cannot work my soul to save,
For that the Lord has done,
But I would work like any slave
For love of God's dear Son.

I have called gratitude for the gospel of grace the
supreme motive for holy living, and so it is. But there is one
more incentive which plays a very important part in the
New Testament. It is the Second Coming of Christ. Into the
details of the doctrine I do not intend to enter here. No
clause of the Creed has suffered more from varieties of interpretation than 'From thence he shall come to judge the
quick and the dead'. Great harm has been done by an un-
warranted dogmatism about the programme of events to
be expected before and after Christ's Return, not to mention the totally unscriptural fixing of dates. What may be
called the Advent certainties are that this present era will
come to its end by the intervention of God, when 'this same
Jesus will come back in the same way as you have seen
him go' (Acts 1.11); that this is a message of hope (Titus
2.13), bringing as it does the assurance of the ultimate
triumph of God when 'the kingdom of the world has become

the kingdom of our Lord and his Christ, and he will reign for ever and ever' (Rev. 11.15); and the certainty of this coming judgment, combined with the uncertainty of the time of it, is a powerful motive to holiness of life.

In what ways does the hope of Christ's Coming spur us to holy living? Chiefly by way of encouragement. The cause of Christ is bound to win. The Christian who seeks to live a godly, righteous and sober life to the glory of God's holy Name in the face of much indifference and opposition is not struggling in vain. The crowning day is coming. So far from despairing and giving up the fight, we redouble our commitment to maintaining 'Christ's quarrel', knowing that the ultimate issue cannot be in doubt. With the Second Coming in view, we live in the light of eternity. There are some striking New Testament passages which bring together the Advent hope and the consequent need for holiness. Thus in 2 Peter 3.11, 12 we read: 'Since everything is coming to an end like this, you should be living holy and saintly lives while you wait and long for the Day of God to come . . . the new heavens and new earth, the place where righteousness will be at home'. Again in 1 John 3.2, 3 : 'All we know is, that when it is revealed we shall be like him because we shall see him as he really is. Surely everyone who entertains this hope must purify himself, must try to be as pure as Christ'.

It is sometimes objected that the introduction of the Second Coming as a motive for holiness brings in the element of reward and punishment, which is considered lower than the motive of love. The hymn attributed to Francis Xavier is quoted :

> My God, I love thee; not because
> I hope for heaven thereby,
> Nor yet because who love thee not
> Are lost eternally.

> Not with the hope of gaining aught,
>   Not seeking a reward;
> But as thyself hast loved me,
>   O ever-loving Lord!

Such sentiments are indeed splendid. But when the New Testament holds out the promise of reward it is not some kind of external happiness which is independent of Christ himself. We might refer to that other medieval hymn which begins –

> Jesu, thou Joy of loving hearts!
> Thou Fount of life! Thou Light of men!

and point out that as we turn to him from the best bliss that *earth* imparts, so there is no bliss that *heaven* affords other than him. If the nature of heavenly rewards is properly understood, I do not think that they can be considered an unworthy incentive.

Unquestionably the prospect of hearing the Master's 'Well done, good and faithful servant' is a part of our Lord's teaching. He was not afraid to use such incentives. The picture he gives of the separation of the sheep and the goats in Matthew 25 shows the Son of Man sitting on his throne of glory and *judging* the nations. The verdict was an intensification of the attitudes they had adopted in this life. Paul takes up the theme of the judgment seat of Christ. He is in no doubt about the salvation of those who are in Christ. 'There is no condemnation for those who are united with Christ Jesus' (Rom. 8.1, N.E.B.) Yet he speaks for himself and all other believers when he says: 'For we must all have our lives laid open before the tribunal of Christ, where each must receive what is due to him for his conduct in the body, good or bad' (2 Cor. 5.10, N.E.B.). There need be no contradiction here. Ultimate salvation is assured through Christ alone, but the judgment of Christ will sort out the value of the Christian life built on this foundation. This is most clearly stated in the passage 1 Cor. 3.11-15. Christ is the foundation. On him we can build with gold, silver and jewels, or with wood, grass and straw. The work of each builder will be clearly revealed when the day comes, the day which is likened to fire. 'If a man's building stands, he will be rewarded; if it burns, he will have to bear the loss; and yet he will escape with his life, as one might from a fire' (verses 14, 15, N.E.B.).

If a word of personal reminiscence may be permitted, I remember vividly a prayer which was said constantly in college chapel asking that we might do our duty, *'remembering the solemn account which we must one day give before the judgment-seat of Christ'*. Those words have remained with me ever since and have been a constant reminder of our accountability to God for the stewardship of our lives. It is but one of a number of motives for holy living, all of which are valid in themselves and overlap with each other. It is perhaps worth remembering that in the history of the Christian Church it has usually been those who have cared most about receiving God's approval who have done most for the good of their fellow-men. A heavenly motive for holiness produces the best earthly results.

Chapter Six

The Experience of Holiness

We have tried to discover what holiness is, how it is shown in daily life, and what are the motives which compel us to seek it. We now need to turn to a consideration of the way in which holiness is to be achieved. Is there a pattern of doctrine given in the New Testament which shows us the way? The Epistles, of course, contain much teaching on the subject. A glance at a concordance reveals that the words 'sanctify', 'sanctified', 'sanctification', occur no less than twenty-three times in the Epistles, in addition to the many references to 'the saints' already mentioned. The words 'holiness' and 'holy' are also frequently to be found, some-times indeed referring to places, or the holy scriptures, but more often to Christian believers. These references are scattered widely through the whole of the New Testament, and it would be possible to construct a systematic theology of holiness by considering them all. There is, however, one New Testament writing which appears to be less of a letter written to meet a special need, and rather more of a doc-trinal treatise, a systematic exposition of God's plan of salvation. That writing is Paul's Letter to the Romans. It deals with man's basic need to be made right with God, with the way of justification by faith in Christ the Saviour, with the life of victory made possible through identification with Christ crucified and risen, a possibility turned into a reality by the power of the Holy Spirit who is himself the pledge of the eternal glory which is the fruition of the new

life. It goes on, in three vital chapters, to speak of God'
world-wide purpose embracing both Jews and Gentiles
before the final exhortation which brings holiness into the
realm of ordinary human situations.

It is the section about the life of victory which chiefly
concerns us now, in other words chapters 5–8. It cannot be
too strongly asserted that only as those who have been de
clared righteous through our faith in the Lord Jesus Christ
can we begin to grasp the life of sanctification which God
wills for us. Justification is the starting point rather than
the goal. But justification, reinstatement into right standing
with God, is not a matter of cold legal transaction : it is
restoration to a warm, personal relationship. The justified
man has peace with God, has access to the enjoyment of
God's friendship, and a joyful anticipation of future glory
Outward circumstances cannot change the reality of the
new life in Christ. Sufferings only serve to develop patience
which in turn brings perseverance, leading to hope of con
tinuing grace. Such hope is based, not on anything in our
selves, but on God's love poured into our hearts by the Holy
Spirit. The measure of that love is seen in the sacrifice of
Christ for us while we were still sinners. His death on the
cross was the decisive act which undid the fatal results of the
fall of man. Adam's sin brought ruin to the world, but
Christ's obedience brings the gift of new life. Yet the gift
is incomparably greater than what has been lost by man'
sin. Isaac Watts wrote in his hymn 'Jesus shall reign' words
which exactly summarize the end of Romans 5 :

> In him the tribes of Adam boast
> More blessings than their father lost.

Paul immediately anticipates the objection which will be
raised : 'Does it follow that we should remain in sin so as to
let grace have greater scope? Of course not' (Rom. 6.1). We

are justified only because we are united to Christ. Our union is with him who died and rose again. When in baptism we were initiated into Christ we also symbolically died in order that we might rise to live a new life. Strong metaphors are used to press home the identification of the believer with Christ. Our former selves have been crucified. The body as the instrument of sin is cancelled out, for death cancels all obligations. But although all this is symbolically true, it has to become actually true in experience. We have to consider ourselves ('reckon yourselves' – A.V.) to be dead to sin, but alive for God in Christ Jesus. It is a case of 'becoming what we are', and involves a continual refusal to allow that sin has any claim, a continual offering of ourselves to God. Paul reinforces the teaching by two illustrations, slavery and marriage. When you were the slaves of sin you were free from righteousness, with terrible consequences. But now, in Christ, you are slaves to God and free from sin, with consequences of sanctification and eternal life. Similarly, a married woman is bound to her husband as long as he is alive. If he dies, she is free to marry another. In this allegory the first husband is our unregenerate nature. This is put to death, and so we are free to be united to Christ in his resurrection life. As long as the 'old man' lives we are under his law. In Christ we are 'free to serve in the new spiritual way and not the old way of a written law' (Rom. 7.6).

God's Law reveals to us the fact of sin, its power, its deceitfulness, its consequences, its exceeding sinfulness. This is happening all the time, and there is always a danger of our returning to the old, unspiritual life. The classic account of the inward conflict given in Romans 7.14–25 is a description, not of an unbeliever, but of a true Christian. Everyone has to learn the truth which Paul knew for himself : 'The fact is, I know of nothing good living in me – living, that is, in my unspiritual self'. So when the struggle

55

is carried on in one's own strength it is bound to end in defeat. I do not believe that this conflict was a stage in Paul's experience which he left behind when he entered into the meaning of Romans 8. It was true of him, as it is of every Christian, whenever he trusted in himself and not in the power of God. It is however when we reach chapter 8 that we find the secret of victorious living, for this is the great passage about the Holy Spirit.

It is only through the work of Christ, dealing with sin and satisfying the demands of the Law, that we are able to 'walk in the Spirit', which is the key to our sanctification. Sanctification brings a complete re-orientation of life. 'The unspiritual are interested only in what is unspiritual, but the spiritual are interested in spiritual things'. Every Christian has the Holy Spirit, for 'unless you possessed the Spirit of Christ you would not belong to him'. The evidence of the Spirit's presence is spirituality, or holiness, a life of being *moved* by the Spirit. Older translations have 'led by the Spirit', but as the Jerusalem Bible note says : ' "led" seem inadequate; the Holy Spirit is much more than one who inwardly admonishes, he is the principle of a life truly divine'. The moving of the Spirit gives us liberty and confidence as God's children. Not that God's children will escape their share of suffering. But suffering enlarges our capacity for that glory which lies before us. The gift of the Spirit is the first-fruits of the redemption one day to be fully enjoyed. Meanwhile the Holy Spirit works in us the will to pray according to the will of God, and gives us the assurance of God's providence and purpose in our lives. Little wonder that Paul ends this section on the way of holiness with an exultant hymn of praise to the unchangeable love of God made visible in Christ Jesus our Lord.

There have been various times in the history of the Church when the rediscovery of a truth has brought an acquisition of new life. The most obvious instance is the doctrine of justification by faith which was the theological cause of the Reformation. Less well known is the new interest in New Testament teaching on sanctification which accompanied the Methodist Revival, and continued through various Holiness Movements. Basically these were neither more nor less than attempts to grasp, and to live by, the teaching which we have just outlined from the Epistle to the Romans. In so far as these movements represent a desire for the greatest possible degree of holiness, and as close a walk with God as is attainable in this present world, they can be nothing but good. The Church can too easily settle down to the mediocrity of mere conformity to outward standards, and needs these sharp reminders of the call of God to the heights. *My Utmost for His Highest,* the title of Oswald Chambers' best-known book, should be the watchword of every Christian. But as always when one doctrine is isolated from the rest of Scripture, there are dangers of distortion, exaggeration, or even error, and at times earnest Christians have not escaped these pitfalls.

John Wesley and the early Methodists laid great stress on such scriptural phrases as 'entire sanctification', 'a clean heart', 'perfect love'. They taught that this was a further stage in the Christian life, a distinctive second blessing to be received subsequent to conversion. There were in fact two classes of Christians, the converted but not sanctified, and the converted and sanctified. That there are some Christians who have entered more fully into their inheritance in Christ than others is patently obvious, but to divide the whole body of Christians into two categories, and the way of entry into two 'blessings', is surely artificial. The Christian believer has all things in Christ. If some experience what seems to be a second blessing, distinct from conversion, this is not because God has previously withheld something, but because the believer has not laid hold of what is his by the gift of God. And when a second experience such as this has

57

taken place there is always more to follow. It is sad if someone, having reached a new level of Christian life, has a feeling of having 'arrived'. Holiness movements have been strewn with the wrecks of those who have laid claim to sinless perfection, and whose lives have belied their profession. I once heard an ardent soul testify that since receiving the second blessing he had enjoyed 'all the fruits of the Spirit'. It must have been the unsanctified part of me which wanted to ask his wife if she could corroborate that claim!

It was the renewed interest in what was called scriptural holiness which led to the founding of the Keswick Convention in 1875. It is an annual event of a week's duration* which today attracts many thousands of Christians for the sole purpose of discovering from the Bible the way of holiness, or as it is often expressed, 'the deepening of the spiritual life'. Keswick is the 'mother' of hundreds of similar conventions all over the world. Its teaching in early years veered towards a second blessing, though it was always explicitly made clear that nothing like sinless perfection was in mind. What is indisputable is that many, who have come to Keswick with the knowledge that their Christian life was less than fully victorious, have gone away with a fresh experience of Christ's power, and a new in-filling of the Holy Spirit, to live a life of faith, and obedience to the will of God, on a level hitherto unknown. Today the emphasis of Keswick is perhaps less on a crisis experience and more on the practical outworking of the holy life, though it needs to be remembered that earlier convention teachers always stressed that the crisis was only the beginning of a process of Christian growth.

One criticism of this movement has been that it so emphasized holiness as a work of God's grace in the life of a believer that it left no room for the equally biblical truth

* A second week has now been added to cater for whole families wishing to combine attendance at the Convention with a holiday.

that human effort is called for. Sometimes the impression may have been given that the human personality is to be so completely quiescent that it is no more than a piece of wire to conduct the electric current of the power of the Holy Spirit. Such lines as these –

> Channels only, blessed Master,
> But with all Thy wondrous power
> Flowing through us, Thou canst use us
> Every day and every hour

can be misleading. The 'channel' is not entirely passive. Human personality is to co-operate actively with the grace of God. Indeed the power of God is not a 'something' which flows into, and through, a person, but the Holy Spirit himself in personal relationship with the believer. Sanctification is the fellowship of the Holy Spirit. He and we together each have our part. Paul brings these two sides together in a single sentence : 'You must work out your own salvation in fear and trembling; for it is God who works in you, inspiring the will and the deed, for his own chosen purpose' (Phil. 2.12, 13. N.E.B.). George Goodman, who was himself a speaker at the Keswick Convention, pointed out the danger of teaching children a chorus which begins 'It is not try, but trust'. He rightly said that it should be 'Try all the harder just because you are trusting'.

Failure to recognize the possible dangers led in the early days to some opposition to holiness movements from those who were themselves no less deeply concerned for true holiness. The most prominent opponent was J. C. Ryle, afterwards the first Bishop of Liverpool. In 1878 he published his book *Holiness,* which is a classic of its kind. The Preface contains seven questions which the author requests his readers to take as *Cautions for the Times.* Here they are : (1) Is it wise to speak of *faith* as the one thing needful

59

. . . in teaching the doctrine of sanctification? . . . that the holiness of converted people is *by faith only, and not at all by personal exertion?* (2) Is it wise to make so little, comparatively, of the many *practical exhortations to holiness in daily life* which are to be found in the Sermon on the Mount, and in the latter part of most of St Paul's epistles? (3) Is it wise to use vague language about *perfection*, and to press on Christians a *standard of holiness*, as attainable in this world, for which there is no warrant to be shown either in Scripture or experience? (4) Is it wise to assert . . . the *the Seventh chapter of the Epistle to the Romans* does not describe the experience of the advanced saint, but the experience of the unregenerate man, or of the weak and unestablished believer? (5) Is it wise to use the language which is often used in the present day about the doctrine of '*Christ in us*'?* (6) Is it wise to draw such a deep, wide, and distinct line of separation between conversion and *consecration, or the higher life, so called*, as many do draw in the present day? (7) Is it wise to teach believers that they ought not to think so much of fighting and struggling against sin, but ought rather to '*yield themselves to God*', and be passive in the hands of Christ? To all these questions Ryle's answer was, 'I doubt it'. Yet his concern was, not to quench the desire for holiness, but rather to keep it practical, and 'according to the proportion of God's Word'. He was at first suspicious of Keswick, fearing its teaching was unbalanced, but by degrees he was reassured, and in 1892 he sat on the speakers' platform along with the American evangelist, D. L. Moody.

Another who started with real misgivings about the Keswick message was Handley C. G. Moule, later to become Bishop of Durham. As Principal of Ridley Hall, Cambridge,

* Ryle fully justifies his apprehension about the use of this scriptural phrase by reference to anitomianism and fanaticism among some who made exaggerated claims.

he was the trusted senior friend of Christian leaders from among the students. He was with them not only in a memorable mission by D. L. Moody, and the going out to China of the Cambridge Seven, but also in a Holiness Convention in which extreme perfectionist views were taught. While Moule welcomed the fervour of spirit, he deplored the erroneous teaching, and was consequently on his guard when he later met the more balanced Keswick teaching. But through the ministry of one of its leaders, the Reverend Evan H. Hopkins, he himself went through a spiritual crisis of faith and self-surrender. Profound New Testament scholar that he was, he became the theologian of the Keswick movement, and no doubt his addresses at the Convention greatly contributed to the balance which Ryle had feared was lacking. He was known affectionately to the students as 'Holy Moule', no doubt greatly to his embarrassment if he ever knew, and few have been so fitted to bear the name. His prolific output of writings, at one and the same time scholarly and devotional, carried his influence far and wide. The Keswick Convention, which he did so much to foster, bears his mark even yet, and having long outgrown the controversies of its early days is still a power for holiness.

If there continue to be varieties of interpretation of scriptural holiness, it is to be hoped that they are not really controversies, but rather differences of opinion. In recent times the ground of these differences has shifted from the nature of sanctification to what are called the charismatic gifts. Unlike the older holiness movements which influenced mainly the evangelicals, the charismatic movement has spread to all sections of the Church. Briefly stated, it stresses the need for Christians to be 'baptized in the Holy Spirit' as a separate and fuller experience in their spiritual life. When this baptism has been received there will usually be the outward evidence of speaking in tongues, a gift which is found helpful thereafter in private devotion. Other gifts, such as healing, may be received, as well the more usual ones of preaching, teaching, administration and the like After being baptized in the Spirit there is said to be a greater love for our Lord, and a much greater freedom of expression in worship, and in loving fellowship with other Christians. Spontaneous joy, with singing and movement, is infectious and accounts for the attractive power of those congregations which claim this new pentecostal blessing. Many who are within the movement would say that this is the way in which the Holy Spirit is reviving the Church today.

There are many earnest Christians who remain critical of this so-called neo-pentecostalism. Some of the dangers inherent in such a movement are obvious, and are often recognized by the leaders themselves. In a congregation or fellowship where some claim to have been baptized in the Spirit and others do not, there is the possibility of serious division, the danger of spiritual pride on the one hand and discouragement on the other. Such division into first and second class Christians has been a potential feature of every spiritual awakening, as for instance in the East African Revival, where actually the Holy Spirit's love and wisdom prevailed, and schism was avoided. In criticism of the pente-costal movement it is sometimes said that there is undue emotion, pressure put on people to respond and let themselves go. This may or may not be a valid judgment, but it is pretty certain that the average worshipping congregation has a lot to learn about the joy of the Lord. Another criticism is that charismatic Christians are over dogmatic in their insistence on the necessity of everyone sharing their views, but if you believe you are right, it is natural that you should want others to come to your point of view. Not all the dogmatism is on one side. Nor, in my experience, is there any monopoly of holiness on one side or the other. In terms of Christ-like character both pentecostals and non-pentecostals produce their saints. No doubt both also produce their share of spiritual casualties.

Much more serious than any of these criticisms is the question whether baptism in the Spirit is taught in Scripture as a second experience apart from conversion, and whether speaking in tongues is the outward sign of its having been received. I am convinced myself that when Paul wrote : 'In the one Spirit we were all baptized, Jews as well as Greeks, slaves as well as citizens, and one Spirit was given to us all to drink' (1 Cor. 12.13), he was addressing the whole Church. We must not belittle the mighty work of God's Spirit when he initiates us into the Body of Christ. This, as I understand the New Testament, is the baptism of the Spirit. Subsequently there may be a further spiritual crisis (rather in the same way that in many churches Confirmation follows after Baptism). There may indeed be many crises, or a more gradual growth, in obedience to the command to be filled with the Spirit. There should certainly be an increasing manifestation of the fruit of the Spirit, as well as an exercise of such gifts of the Spirit as he bestows in answer to prayer and faith. That the gift of tongues is an essential mark of having received the Holy Spirit I find it impossible to maintain in the face of Scripture, history and experience.*

In the end the test of Scripture must be decisive. I have suggested that we all have much to learn from Christians of the charismatic outlook, and I am sure this is true. I believe also that they have much to learn from others, not least in bringing everything under the judgment of the Word of God. I am sure that many are doing this, but there are still excesses which discredit the movement, and may have the unfortunate effect of frightening some away from any further search for a deeper experience of the Holy Spirit. This is tragic, for the greatest need of the Church is

* For a full treatment of this subject see *Spiritual gifts and the church*, Donald Bridge and David Phypers, Inter-Varsity Press.

a renewal of its inward life of holiness, which is possible only by the Spirit's power. The call to all who seek this renewal, whatever their presuppositions, is for humility before God and one another, and openness to his truth which is revealed in the Bible. This way lies true unity. In this connection some words of J. C. Ryle, in the Preface already quoted, are applicable to us all. 'I plead that a movement in favour of holiness cannot be advanced by new coined phraseology, or by disproportioned and one-sided statements – or by overstraining and isolating particular texts – or by exalting one truth at the expense of another – or by allegorizing and accommodating texts, and squeezing out of them meanings which the Holy Ghost never put in them – or by speaking contemptuously and bitterly of those who do not entirely see things with our eyes, and do not work exactly in our ways. These things do not make for peace : they rather repel many and keep them at a distance. The cause of true sanctification is not helped, but hindered by such weapons as these. A movement in aid of holiness which produces strife and dispute among God's children is somewhat suspicious. For Christ's sake, and in the name of truth and charity, let us endeavour to follow after peace as well as holiness. "What God has joined together let no man put asunder".'

Chapter Seven

The Means of Grace

In his book on John Wesley's doctrine of holiness, *The Path to Perfection*, W. E. Sangster wrote :

> 'There is an experience of God the Holy Spirit, available
> for all who will seek it with importunity, which imparts
> spiritual power far above the level enjoyed by the average
> Christian : which inspires a caring God-like love different
> in kind from the affections of normal nature : which
> communicates to the eager soul the penetrating power of
> holiness. No book can give this experience. It belongs
> to the secret intercourse of the soul with God. It lies
> at the very heart of personal religion. Its wide reception
> would transform the Church and shake the world. . . .
> Faith and prayer are the ordained means, and progress
> may be measured by one's progress in humility.'*

Whatever facet of the doctrine of sanctification makes its
special appeal to us, all Christians agree that the Holy Spirit
is the author of holiness; that while holiness is spiritual
power and deep love it is also characterized by humility; and
that the means whereby it is obtained is faith and prayer. I
take the word prayer in its widest possible connotation, to
include every kind of devotional activity, both private and
public, individual and corporate. Holiness is the gift of
God's grace, and we are now to consider the means of grace.
It is certain we shall not grow in grace unless we use the
means.

* p. 7.

Dr Sangster is right when he says that no book can give the experience of holiness. Neither can a book teach us to pray. It is however interesting to note that the many books that have been written on the subject seem to transcend the differences which divide Christians in other ways. John Wesley greatly valued a book of devotions by John Austin, a Roman Catholic, and issued his own edition of it in his Christian Library of Practical Divinity. Christians of many different traditions have learned to pray with the Anglican Lancelot Andrewes, as they do today with the Roman Catholic Michel Quoist. We cannot afford to miss any possible source of help. But it is perfectly true that the experience of prayer can only be won by praying. We, no less than the disciples, need to make the request : 'Lord, teach us to pray' (Luke 11.1). It was when they had seen Jesus at prayer that they realized their own need for help and guidance. Perhaps the first step in the art of learning to pray is to admit our ignorance and ask to be taught.

The immediate answer to the disciples' petition was to be given the form of words which we call the Lord's Prayer. But this is far more than a set form to be used *verbatim*; it is also a model for all our praying. In our ignorance we may over-emphasize one particular aspect of prayer. A popular idea, for instance, is that prayer consists mainly in asking things for oneself or others, and when these are not granted in the way people hope they too easily give up praying altogether. The Lord's Prayer shows us that the most important part of our devotional life is concerned with the worship of God, the coming of his Kingdom, the doing of his will. Before ever we begin to ask God for our daily bread – and the inclusion of this petition as the first request for ourselves teaches that God is interested in every aspect of our earthly life – we are first to become adjusted to our heavenly Father, to acknowledge him as the Holy One, to see the world, and ourselves within it, from his viewpoint.

and to align our wills with his. For most of us this will mean giving ourselves time to be quiet, and to concentrate. Many find it helpful to begin with a few verses of the Bible, some passage which lifts our minds to God himself, such as Isaiah 6.1–5; or to picture some scene from one of the Gospels in which Jesus reveals the character of the Father. When it comes to putting our worship into words, some parts of the Psalms, or of hymns of adoration, may be useful. But we may find words are not necessary at all. Perhaps no command is less frequently obeyed than that in Psalm 46.10 R.S.V. : 'Be still, and know that I am God'.

There is a sense in which, in thus worshipping the Lord, we forget ourselves. This does not come easily to self-conscious adults. I like the story of the mother who rebuked her small son for some misdemeanour, saying, 'Come, come, you forget yourself'. The boy replied : 'Don't you wish *you* could?' We need to become so absorbed with God that we cease to be at the centre of our thoughts. Indeed, if we truly worship, we shall begin to see ourselves in all our unworthiness and sinfulness, as Isaiah did, and cry out for God's forgiveness. Penitence is a part of true prayer, and the holiest people have always been most conscious of their sins. But penitence is not morbid introspection. It is to lead to the glad acceptance of forgiveness from God and a forgiving spirit to others, and surrender to the guidance of God, away from the things which cause us to sin, and towards the path of deliverance. These gifts of God must inevitably cause us to thank and praise him. Somehow thanksgiving to God – just saying thank you to him for specific things that he has given – is a neglected part of prayer. As with worship, thanksgiving can be helped by psalms and hymns. As Paul advised : 'Sing the words and tunes of the psalms and hymns when you are together, and go on singing and chanting to the Lord in your hearts, so that always and everywhere you are giving thanks to God who is our Father in the name of our Lord Jesus Christ' (Eph. 5.19, 20). Neither need thanksgiving be limited to those circumstances which are obviously helpful. There is profound wisdom in the words seen on a motto-card : 'Hallelujah anyway !'

In stressing the importance of these aspects of prayer, I have no desire to belittle the need and the value of petition and intercession. There are great difficulties in understanding how the doing of God's will can be dependent on our praying. Certainly God does not need to be reminded, or persuaded, to do what he most wants to do. But God has chosen to work through human co-operation. Just as he uses the proclamation of the gospel by a human evangelist to draw someone to himself, so he has chosen to use the praying of his people to accomplish his purpose. It is sometimes said that when we pray it is not the circumstances or people we are praying for that change, but we ourselves. This I believe to be only a part of the truth. Undoubtedly, as we pray, we change in relation to the object of our prayer. But Scripture makes it clear, and experience bears out, that prayer changes things as well. Peter was imprisoned by Herod. 'All the time Peter was under guard the Church prayed to God for him unremittingly' (Acts 12.5). The result was not simply that Peter was comforted, or that the Church was strengthened to endure the time of testing. The result was that the prison doors were opened, the chains fell from his hands, and Peter was a free man. Modern miracles in answer to prayer are far too numerous to be mere coincidence. It is natural to think of some of the outstanding examples like Hudson Taylor, the founder of the China Inland Mission (now the Overseas Missionary Fellowship), and George Müller and his Orphanage. In both cases the money and personnel for the work were never sought by appeal to men, but only by prayer to God, and the history of both enterprises abounds in stories of thrilling answers.

But these well-known cases can be matched by the experience of thousands of more ordinary Christians who have known beyond doubt that God answers prayer, not just in a subjective way, but by changing things. Moreover those who have prayed most have been those who are least concerned over the supposed difficulties about intercession.

It follows that a mature prayer life will grow, not only in depth, but in breadth. Most people begin praying with a very limited horizon, and some alas, advance very little. Lancelot Andrewes' *Preces Privatae* reveal a man whose devotion was deep and his intercession wide. In our age we have no excuse for not making our prayers world-wide in scope. Literature about the work of the Church in all the world is available, and daily papers and news bulletins keep us up-to-date with world events. We should be able to pray with real understanding. To cover a wide field requires some kind of system, as is provided by various cycles of prayer on a monthly or weekly basis, but particular interests will have their special appeal to an individual for daily and more detailed intercession. Prayer for others, like the worship of God, takes us out of ourselves, and he who intercedes most is likely to grow most in holiness.

In what I have written so far I have been thinking about private prayer, but this is only one way of using this means of grace. There is prayer in the worship of the Church, whether of a liturgical or of a freer pattern. Perhaps some who find a liturgy unhelpful need to be reminded that such prayers provide a standard of devotion independent of the ability or spirituality of a particular minister. Many of the ancient prayers have stood the test of centuries and seem to stretch our spirits as we try to make them our own. Of course they can become formal, as no doubt the liturgical prayers of the synagogue sometimes were when our Lord attended the services. Perhaps those most wedded to liturgical forms need to learn more of the spontaneous freedom of extempore prayer. There is much to be said for small groups of committed Christians meeting together informally for intercession. At times of spiritual awakening this has generally happened, and the multiplication of such prayer meetings is one of the hopeful signs today. Even more than the larger gatherings of the church on a weekday for intercession – which is very desirable – the smaller meetings, where members get to know each other very well, seem to provide an opportunity to grow in the prayer life, helped on by mutual encouragement. And there is one group which is small enough, and ought to be united enough, to pray together every day – the family. The once prevalent Family Worship, after a period of near extinction, is now happily reviving.

Closely associated with prayer is the reading and study of the Bible. I have already mentioned the use of passages of Scripture in our devotions. Prayer is two-way traffic, like the angels on Jacob's ladder going up and coming down. We need to listen to God's voice from heaven, and the way to be sure that what we hear is not just our own fancy is to check everything by the written Word of God. Indeed God normally speaks to us through his Word. That is not to say that we can treat the Bible unintelligently, as if it were a book of magic or a collection of isolated texts. We need to be able to relate a passage of Scripture to its context, and to interpret it in the light of the whole. Spiritual growth is fostered by a thorough knowledge of the Bible. It goes without saying that preaching in the Church should be based on robust exposition of Scripture. Topical talks or moral essays are a poor substitute for the ministry of the Word. A Bible-based message is always up-to-date, and speaks to the heart and conscience of the hearer. It is my belief that the Sunday ministry should be supplemented by Bible teaching of some kind during the week.

'Every man a Bible student' may be a remote ideal, though

the slogan was first used, not for a sophisticated congregation of university men, but for those East African Christians who had been influenced by the revival. At any rate it has normally been assumed that a Christian should be a Bible *reader*, even if not a student. For many years there have been available shemes of reading, with notes adapted to the needs of various age-groups, almost always based on the assumption of *daily* reading. The Scripture Union and the Bible Reading Fellowship are the two best known organizations. No doubt the ideal for most people is to conform to this habit. I believe, however, that there is danger in too legalistic an attitude to Bible-reading. Not only do people vary enormously in their mental ability to grasp the meaning of words, but their whole way of life may make it, either comparatively easy, or else virtually impossible, to read the Scriptures meaningfully every day. For some the best way may be to meet together with others for a longer period once a week in order to master the Scriptures. I would plead that we should not cling to one method as if it were the only one. Nevertheless for very many Christians the daily reading and pondering of the Scriptures is the best way.

Traditionally the devotional period of Bible reading, meditation and prayer has been the first activity of the day. Variously called the Quiet Time or the Morning Watch, it has been associated with the virtue of early rising. I have before me as I write a manual for young communicants written in 1903 by Robert Charles Joynt, one of the great pastors of his day. In it he writes : 'The best time for your Bible is the early hours of the morning. The house is still, and you are secure, as a rule, against interruption. It honours God when he is given the first place in our day's programme. . . . No one who is in good health ought to be in bed after six o'clock till they pass the prime of their life'. The biographies of saintly people usually tell a similar story : Charles Simeon, for instance, rose at four for his devotions.

Times have changed, the pace of life is much faster, but one sometimes wonders if the present generation has lost something of the discipline of our fathers. It may not be possible to spend several hours – or even a single hour – each day, as once seems to have been fairly common, but can there be any real growth in holiness when all that is offered for this purpose is ten minutes? Time must be found, sufficient time to enable us to be unhurried. It cannot be in the early morning for everybody, and we must avoid making a fetish out of what may be an ideal for some. Different hours of the day will suit the housewife, the office worker, the farmer, the student. Some are more able to concentrate at night than in the morning, others can take time at midday.

Concentration on the importance of a Quiet Time is not an end in itself. Paul's command to the Thessalonians is to pray constantly, which suggests that throughout our conscious hours we should be aware of God's nearness, and able at any moment to speak to him. Such ejaculatory prayers may consist of only a word or two : 'Lord, help me !' 'Father, thank you', 'Lord, I love you'. For long stretches of time our thoughts must be occupied with our daily work, our social conversations, our family affairs. It is not necessary consciously to 'say a prayer' about every detail in order to be doing all to the glory of God. Someone once asked Hudson Taylor if we could be aware that we were always abiding in Christ. He replied that it was more important that we should never be aware that we are *not* abiding in Christ. The presence of God and our relationship with him can be the background of our whole life. But undoubtedly this experience is made more possible by the faithful observance of periods of quiet, and frequent 'arrow' prayers throughout the day.

Even when the Christian is most alone in his private devotions, he is still a member of Christ's Church, aware of his one-ness with all other Christians the world over, and indeed with those who have gone before. The model prayer begins, not *My* Father, but *Our* Father. The Holy Spirit who brings us to acknowledge Christ our Lord at the same time makes us members of his Body. When we pray, therefore, we pray not only *for* our fellow-believers, but *with* them, and are made aware of our dependence on the prayers of others. This is of enormous help when we go through periods of spiritual dryness, as we all do. We may think we are praying badly – though the apparent barrenness of our prayers may be God's way of teaching us to persevere irrespective of our feelings – and then we remember that the whole Church is praying with us. But this sense of togetherness needs to be fostered by actually meeting with our fellow-Christians in worship and genuinely open fellowship. We cannot be in love and charity with people we scarcely know. Hence the vital importance for holiness of meaningful membership of the Church, and of the sacrament of Holy Communion which expresses it. For at the Lord's Table we not only remember his death till he come, so strengthening our love and our hope; we not only feed on Christ in our hearts by faith, so increasing our trust and confidence in him; we not only give thanks for all that he has done for our salvation, and offer our souls and bodies to him for his service; but we also partake of the one bread and drink of the one cup, and so express our one-ness in Christ and our love for one another. Such fellowship is a means of grace without which there can be no true holiness. What is expressed in the Holy Communion needs to be worked out in the details of our lives.

Chapter Eight

The Urge to Evangelize

In a Mission to Oxford University William Temple once said : 'Christ's gift of himself, that is to say of perfect love is not something you can have and keep. If you are keeping it, it proves you have not got it'. In other words, it is of the nature of the gospel that it is received to be passed on. Those who have bathed in the Dead Sea will know that, interesting as the experience may be, the water is most unpleasant. For the Dead Sea is constantly receiving water from the Jordan but there is no outlet at the other end. The water just evaporates, leaving its deposit of salts. That is why it is 'dead' : there is no outlet. Very different is a swim in the Lake of Galilee where all the time water flows in at the north and out at the south. It is cool and refreshing. There is life. It is essential to holiness that the channel of intake and the channel of outflow be alike kept unblocked, otherwise there will be stagnation. Unless there is a willingness to bear witness to others there is little evidence of spiritual life at all. Profession of faith is the outward expression of the inward commitment of the heart. 'If your lips confess that Jesus is Lord and if you believe in your heart that God raised him from the dead, then you will be saved' (Rom. 10. 9). We could indeed have included this subject in the last chapter as one of the means of grace, for it is certain we shall not grow in holiness, unless we are constantly giving out as well as taking in.

Holiness entails obedience to the will of God. Christ's command to 'go and make disciples of all the nations' is as

inding on the whole church for all time as is his command
o 'do this in remembrance of me'. Clearly not every member of the Church is called to preach. 'There is a variety
of gifts but always the same Spirit' (1 Cor. 12.4). Every
Christian is to use what gift he has been given for building
up the body of Christ. Some are apostles, some prophets,
some evangelists, some pastors and teachers (see Eph. 4.11).
But there are also administrators, alms-givers, officials, and
those who do works of mercy (Rom. 12.7, 8). Along one or
more of these channels the life of the Spirit is to flow out to
others. Whatever the form of service, unless it is accompanied by a consistent life it will not be truly effective. The
emphasis throughout our discussion has been that 'being'
is even more important than 'doing'. But we cannot escape
the obligation to use the gifts God has given in the service
of the gospel. This means being where the people are,
going out to them in friendship and loving concern. Lay
people need to be reminded that they have opportunities in
their daily life which no clergyman or minister can share.
Indeed it is a large part of the task of the clergy to equip
the laity for the work of witnessing. Witness includes not
only direct evangelistic approach and personal caring, but
involvement in the social needs of our neighbourhood and
of the whole world. Our Lord's parable of the good Samaritan leaves us in no doubt about who is our neighbour, or
about the obligation of everyone to go and do the same.
Part of our concern can be expressed by personal service,
but this is inevitably limited. What we can do in our little
sphere must be supplemented by encouraging others, giving
that others may serve, influencing public opinion, and above
all by prayer.

The concept of the serving Church, the involvement of
Christian people in the needs of the world, has come very
much to the fore in recent years. One would almost be led
at times to think it was a new discovery. But it is difficult to

imagine how followers of our Lord Jesus Christ could eve[r]
lose sight of the role of the servant. 'Here am I among yo[u]
as one who serves!' said Jesus, and even if he had neve[r]
spoken the words, his life was all the evidence needed. I[n]
point of fact Christians have no need to be ashamed of th[e]
record of the Church in education and medicine, in th[e]
social crusade for the improvement of the lot of all man[-]
kind, in the struggle to get men to care for the hungry, th[e]
homeless and the destitute. Kathleen Heasman in he[r]
Evangelicals in Action* has shown how this was true o[f]
the nineteenth century. In an exhaustive study of the socia[l]
work done by the Evangelicals she paints the picture of des[-]
perate need, and of sacrificial service to meet it. From score[s]
of names and causes we can pick out a few which speak fo[r]
themselves : Wilberforce and the abolition of the slave trade[,]
Shaftesbury and the Ragged School Union, Barnardo an[d]
destitute children, Josephine Butler and the reform o[f]
prostitutes, Elizabeth Fry and prison reform. Add to thes[e]
the movements for the care of the blind and the deaf, th[e]
unsound in mind and body, the sick and aged, and man[y]
others in need. It is reckoned that a good three-quarters o[f]
the voluntary societies which exploded into being in th[e]
nineteenth century were Evangelical in character. In othe[r]
words, all this work for the social and material welfare o[f]
mankind was undertaken by people whose caring was th[e]
overflowing of the love of God.

It would be unfair to suggest that this wave of service t[o]
humanity had no weaknesses, or that all godly people
automatically threw in their lot with it. Some words o[f]
Josephine Butler are a cautionary tale for any age : 'The
godly people have numerous conferences for the deepening
of the spiritual life, from which they come away gorged with
spiritual foodstuff. What is the use of these conferences when
they result in nothing and leave the hell around as bad a[s]

* Geoffrey Bles, 1962.

ver?' Nor is it fair to suggest that the spirit of service is lacking among Christians today. Much of what was pioneered by voluntary bodies is now the responsibility of the state or the local authority, and many committed Christians work within the statutory service. And there are still many areas which are not covered by official agencies. Within and without the state system, thousands of Christian people are caring for the aged and the little children, the delinquents and the drug-addicts, the deprived and the destitute. It often involves great sacrifice and is emphatically the outflowing of the love of God. It is holiness in action. And it is evangelism.

For evangelism is proclaiming the evangel, the good news. The gospel declares that Christ came in order that men 'may have life and have it to the full' (John 10.10). Such a claim undoubtedly has social implications. As Jesus cared for men's bodies, so must his followers. The love of God must be shared irrespective of whether it evokes any response. When our Lord healed ten men of leprosy only one showed any gratitude. Yet we instinctively know that he was right to heal them all. So also are we right to go on serving mankind, and thereby showing them God's love, whether they evidence any interest in the message of the gospel or not. What we try to do for others must be done out of love for them and not merely as a bait, to catch an unwary fish. But here we need to think very clearly. Love wants to share the highest and best things we have. Therefore a Christian, however much he is willing to serve others in any way they consciously seem to need, cannot stop short of wanting to share the greatest treasure he possesses, which is the knowledge of Christ. It is not a case of loving people in order to break down their resistance so that we can speak to them of our Lord. It is rather a matter of loving them without limit so that we cannot be satisfied until we have presented Christ to them.

Neither personal piety on the one hand, nor social concern on the other, nor for that matter both of them together are an adequate expression of holiness. There must be a real desire to bring people to know Christ. Our forefathers used expressions like 'soul-winning', and talked about having 'passion for souls'. We have seen that this did not mean that they neglected the social implications of the gospel but did mean that they had things in perspective. We desperately need to recover the eternal dimension in our message and in our living. As Bishop Stephen Neill has written : 'A salvation which is conceived in purely three-dimensional terms ends by being no salvation at all'.* The New Testament sees people without Christ as lost and needing the eternal life which Christ came to bring. 'You shall give him the name Jesus (Saviour), for he will save his people from their sins' (Matt. 1.21. N.E.B.). As the early Christians began to experience the power of this saving name, we find that they preached Christ as the only way of salvation. Peter declared : 'For of all the names in the world given to men, this is the only one by which we can be saved' (Acts 4.12). The saving name is also the exclusive name. Such exclusiveness has been called intolerance and bigotry over against the current fashion of syncretism. But whatever we call it, this is the New Testament position. Christ's claim is no less : 'I am the Way, the Truth and the Life. No one can come to the Father except through me'. It is this conviction which makes missionaries. The saving and exclusive name becomes also the motivating name : 'It was entirely for the sake of the name that they set out' (3 John 7).

The obligation of the whole Church to carry the gospel to the whole world has often been discharged with lukewarmness, and has sometimes met with opposition. In so far as the opposition is due to ignorance it may be overcome by education. People need to be taught that the Church's

* Article : 'Salvation Today?' *The Churchman*, Winter 1973.

mission to the world is not simply philanthropy but evangelism. The gospel is to be presented not just to the underprivileged of the developing countries, but to every sinner in the world. A high standard of living, with all that is best in education, medicine and technology, does not make bad men good. It does not even make men happy and secure, bring peace to families and neighbourhoods, remove anxiety and fear, let alone turn sinners into saints and give them the assurance of eternal life. Only the gospel can do that. And the gospel carries within itself the obligation of mission. If Jesus is Lord, he is Lord of all. 'The missionary motive of the Church', writes Jakób Jocz, 'cannot be her will for expansion or her desire to compete with other religions. No philanthropic sentiment, no cultural impulse, no political expediency such as the unification of the world, can validate Christian missions. The only justification for the missionary enterprise is faith in the Lordship of Jesus Christ. If the Church really believes that Jesus is Lord, then she can be nothing else than a missionary Church, otherwise she trifles with her profession.'*

Unfortunately opposition to the missionary obligation is not always due to ignorance of these things. There is a theological point of view, seriously put forward, which amounts to saying that Christ is not the only way. I do not think anyone would wish to dispute the fact that there is a degree of truth in non-Christian religions, but that all religions lead ultimately to the same knowledge of God is quite another matter, and is contradicted by the claims of Christ himself. The quotation just given from Dr Jocz is of special interest because he himself is a Hebrew Christian. If any religion could be regarded as outside the scope of Christian witness, surely it would be the Jews. Certainly any Christian of sensitivity can only think of a Jew with gratitude for all that has been received through the Old Testament reve-

* *Christians and Jews,* S.P.C.K. 1966, p. 8.

lation, and especialy for Jesus whom the New Testament calls 'the glory of your people Israel' as well as 'a light to enlighten the pagans' (Luke 2.32). To that gratitude must be added a sense of shame for the way Christians have treated Jews at many times throughout history. But if we believe that Jesus is Lord we must believe that he is Lord of all. We cannot make exceptions of any, not even (or perhaps I should say, least of all) those to whom Jesus first came. 'Between Church and Synogogue', says Jocz, 'there is only one issue – the claim which the Church makes on behalf of Jesus Christ.'* And again : 'Only in confrontation with the Synagogue does the centrality of Jesus Christ for the Christian faith become truly visible'.†

This is not an unnecessary digression in a book about holiness. Holiness cannot be separated from the urge to evangelize, and evangelism is bringing Christ to all men who do not know him. It is significant that, *pace* the words of Josephine Butler quoted above, movements for the encouragement of holiness have also promoted the cause of evangelism. The Salvation Army is a case in point. From its foundation it had a strong message of holiness, with a doctrine akin to Wesley's emphasizing entire sanctification and the clean heart. Its Sunday morning gatherings, intended for the edification of members rather than reaching outsiders, were known as Holiness Meetings. But holiness was never allowed to remain an inward personal experience. It led men and women, sometimes with very little in the way of natural endowment, to go out into the world to testify to Christ and, in the words of their General, 'go for souls, and go for the worst'. The amazing achievements in social welfare, by which the Salvation Army is best known today, go hand in hand with the urge to evangelize; and both are the outcome of their emphasis on holiness. The same was true

* p. 8.
† p. 12.

t an earlier date of the little band of men known as the Clapham Sect. Deep devotion to our Lord, evidenced in prayer and Bible study, witness and service, led not only to the terrific crusade which ended with the abolition of the slave trade, but also to the founding of the Church Missionary Society in 1799.

In the earliest days of the Keswick Convention no place was found in the programme for a specific missionary meeting. But very soon the principle was clearly enunciated that 'consecration and the evangelization of the world ought to go together'. From then on, the missionary note has never been omitted. It would be quite impossible to calculate the impact of the Keswick movement on world evangelization. As a result of deepened spiritual life hundreds – indeed thousands – have been called to service, the prayer-life of multitudes has been quickened, and broadened to take in intercession for the whole world, and vast sums of money have been contributed for the spread of the gospel. The Church Missionary Society itself experienced a tremendous increase from 1887 onwards, trebling its number of missionaries within twelve years, and receiving all the money needed to send and support them. Eugene Stock, the historian of the Society, saw that this forward movement was intimately connected with a deep revival of the spiritual life, and the teaching of a higher standard of devotion to the Lord Jesus. Let the Holy Ghost himself stir the heart and enlighten the eyes, and the conversion of the unconverted becomes a matter of anxious concern. And so we have seen in these pages how much the modern development of missions owes to the spiritual movements of the day.'*

Not for one moment would I suggest that the missionary task has not changed almost beyond recognition since the time of which I have written. No longer can we think of 'sending' churches and 'receiving' churches. Every country

The History of the Church Missionary Society. Vol. III, p. 804.

is a mission field, and the Church in each needs the help c
all. But the basic need for every Christian to think in term
of global strategy remains the same. We must live witl
our windows open to the wind of the Spirit from whateve
direction. The metaphor does not suggest a life of ease an
comfort, but such a life is not part of the Christian calling
It is quite certain that the Spirit will reveal the will of Go
for each life, and that many who respond to his prompting
will find themselves in situations which call for pioneering
though usually in a different sense from our forefather
The degree of dedication required is no less when the jungl
is concrete. There are of course still areas where the peopl
are primitive, and languages into which the Scriptures hav
not yet been translated. God calls some to such work. Man
more are called to serve an already existing Church, offerin
such gifts and skills as may be asked for. The work is one th
world over, and the need for workers exists everywhere. Th
chief qualification is holiness.

I have already referred to the Jews as a test case i
determining whether the gospel is of universal applicatior
If there were to be any exception, it would be they. On th
other hand we remember that the Apostles and all the firs
Christians were Jews, that they found in Jesus, not a
alien figure, but one of themselves, the culmination of th
revelation given by God, to whom the Old Testamen
Scriptures bear witness. Paul, who described himself as
Hebrew of the Hebrews, became the Apostle to the Gentile
He was the first to understand and develop fully the trut
that in Christ the old barriers between Jew and Gentil
were done away. Nevertheless in his missionary journey
he seems always to have gone first to the synagogue. An
in Romans 9.10 and 11, where he works out in detail th
relationship of Israel as the Chosen People to the Church c
Christ, he uses language which suggests that the Jews ar
still a priority in Christian thinking. They are still God

chosen people, for 'God never takes back his gifts or revokes his choice' (11.29). He sees their rejection of Christ as the cutting off of branches of an olive tree, in order that shoots of wild olive (Gentiles) might be grafted in (11.17). But he adds that 'God is perfectly able to graft them back again; after all, if you were cut from your natural wild olive to be grafted unnaturally on to a cultivated olive, it will be much easier for them, the natural branches, to be grafted back on the tree they came from' (11.24). In other words he foresees the time when the Jews will acknowledge Jesus. And this will be a day of enrichment for the whole world. 'Think of the extent to which the world, the pagan world, has benefited from their fall and defection – then think how much more it will benefit from the conversion of them all' (11.12).

In short, God's purpose in Christ will not be complete until his own Chosen People are brought in, and when that happens there will be blessing in all the world on a scale hitherto unknown.* This is typical of Paul's optimism. He knows that the ultimate issue is not in any doubt. However long delayed, the triumph of Christ must come. The saving name, which is the exclusive name and the motivating name, is also the victorious name.

> God raised him high
> and gave him the name
> which is above all other names
> so that all beings
> in the heavens, on earth and in the underworld,
> shall bend the kneee at the name of Jesus
> and every tongue should acclaim
> Jesus Christ as Lord,
> to the glory of God the Father.

* For a full discussion of this view, widely taught in many parts of the Church, see *The Puritan Hope* by Iain Murray, The Banner of Truth Trust.

With such a prospect, who can fail to be optimistic? Th
hope of glory is not the selfish anticipation of individual jo
in heaven. It is the certainty of the victory of Christ'
Kingdom. Such a hope gives urgency to our evangelisti
task.

Chapter Nine

The Way Forward

We finished the last chapter on a note of hope. The triumph of Christ and his Kingdom is assured in the very nature of the case. The Church is the instrument of the coming of the Kingdom which cannot fail. In his great passage on the Resurrection, Paul says : 'For he must be king until he has put all his enemies under his feet' (1 Cor. 15.25). It is true, as the writer to the Hebrews says, 'At present we are not able to see that everything has been put under his command, but we do see in Jesus one who was for a short while made lower than the angels and *is now crowned with glory and splendour* (Heb. 2.8, 9). The victory was won through the suffering of the cross. As William Temple put it : 'The date of the triumph of love is Good Friday, not Easter Day. Yet if the story had ended there, the victory would have been barren. What remains is not to win it, but to gather in its fruits'.* With the loud cry, 'It is finished', the victory was complete. 'He was proclaimed Son of God in all his power through his resurrection from the dead' (Rom. 1.4). In the arresting words of 1 John 3.8 : 'It was to undo all that the devil had done that the Son of God appeared'.

The context of that last quotation shows that the reference is not just to the final triumph of Christ's Kingdom to be manifested at the last day, but to the personal holiness of each individual believer. Yet in a sense the two are one. Christ's Kingdom is the Kingdom of holiness and its coming can only be through holy people. Conversely, as we have

* *Readings in St John's Gospel*, p. 375.

seen when discussing motives for holiness, the certainty of the final victory of Christ is a spur to individual sanctity. The optimism, which Scripture encourages us to cling to with regard to the whole issue of the Kingdom, can apply to ourselves and our own growth in grace. 'I am quite certain', writes Paul to the Christians at Philippi, 'that the One who began this good work in you will see that it is finished when the Day of Christ Jesus comes' (Phil. 1.6). Charles Wesley has expressed the Christian hope thus :

> Finish then thy new creation,
>   Pure and spotless let us be;
> Let us see thy great salvation,
>   Perfectly restored in thee;
> Changed from glory into glory
>   Till in heaven we take our place;
> Till we cast our crowns before thee,
>   Lost in wonder, love, and praise.

So in thinking of the way forward, we begin with the goal to which we are moving. The future of the Kingdom, of the Church, and of the individual believer, is not in doubt. The gates of hell shall not prevail.

Alongside the truth of the future glory when at last Christ reigns must be placed the equally certain fact that the path to glory is the way of the cross. The history of the Church has been one of conflict with the forces of sin. Often there has been compromise, sometimes downright treachery, at best a half-hearted engagement in the struggle. The marvel is that the Church remains, in spite of itself, the instrument of God in the world. We are still, in Bishop Frank Houghton's words,

> Facing a task unfinished,
> That drives us to our knees,
> A need that, undiminished,
> Rebukes our slothful ease,

hough realism compels us to admit that, while the Church's unfinished task rebukes our slothful ease, it far too seldom drives us to our knees.

There remains the unfinished task, not only of the evangelization of the world and the establishment of the crown rights of the Redeemer in every area of life, but also in the sanctification of very individual Christian. Paul could write with great assurance of his position in Christ and of the future glory that lay before him (2 Tim. 4.7, 8). But he was equally obliged to write: 'Not that I have become perfect yet: I have not yet won, but I am still running, trying to capture the prize for which Christ Jesus captured me. I can assure you my brethren, I am far from thinking that I have already won. All I can say is that I forget the past and I strain ahead for what is still to come; I am racing for the finish, for the prize to which God calls us upwards to receive in Christ Jesus' (Phil. 3.12–14). Here speaks not one who thinks of himself as having 'arrived', but who is straining every nerve to win through. The future for him, right up to the gate of heaven, was to be one of conflict. Equally will it be for us.

I do not believe that the way of holiness is either more or less difficult than it was in the earliest days of the Church. The problems were different in their outward manifestations, but they were basically the same. The world, the flesh and the devil only change very superficially, and the problem of living a life of loyalty to Christ's perfect standards is as great today as it was then. Certainly I do not think that, for all the changes we have seen within even the last fifty years, the basic things have altered very much from our fathers' times. Much of the tradition I have been outlining in the preceding chapters was hammered out within the past two hundred years. No doubt the life-style of Christians has changed in that period, as has the life-style of society in general. But I believe it will be found that changes have been in non-esentials. After all we, like our forefathers should be slaves to the Word of God, and if we can get behind the traditions which have been handed down to us stripping them of what is of merely transitory value, we shall come to see that holiness, like our Lord who inspires it, is the same yesterday, and today, and for ever.

This is emphatically not to deny that the holy life has to be lived in circumstances which our fathers never knew. The Christian has to decide his attitudes to new questions such as world poverty, abortion, euthanasia, the mass media, just as former generations dealt with slavery and vice, and as Paul had to sort out the problems of Christians living amid the moral degradation of Corinth. But basically the conflict is the same as it always has been, the struggle to maintain Christ's absolute standards of love, truth, unselfishness and purity. These are the 'four absolutes' which were the basis of the Oxford Group Movement, now known as Moral Re-Armament. I have always thought the Movement to be lacking in an adequate theology of salvation – though this is no criticism of particular people within it whom I have known to be sincere Christians – but I cannot see how any Christian could object to the 'absolutes'. They are, in fact, taken directly from our Lord's Sermon on the Mount. I am not sure that we ought not to add a fifth, absolute humility, but this may well be included in absolute love. I believe we all need the challenge of these absolutes, and my fear is that some of the changes in life-style which we notice among Christians today are not just adaptations to the needs and problems of contemporary society, but rather the lowering of standards under pressure from the world around us. We must not be bound by the taboos and traditions of the past, but let us be quite sure that what we put in their place are genuine improvements. We must learn to distinguish between changing patterns and unchanging principles.

If we are searching for the way of holiness for the last

quarter of the twentieth century, I think I find a clue in the various movements of the present time which we have discussed in previous chapters. Not only do they all have something to contribute, but they act as checks one to the other. Perhaps it may be, as Charles Simeon said of the Calvinist–Arminian controversy which was so divisive in the Church of his day, that the truth lies, not between the two extremes, but at both extremes. I think we must learn to take all the help we can, from whatever source. Paul's advice is very relevant : 'Do not quench the Spirit, do not despise prophesying, but test everything; hold fast what is good, abstain from every form of evil' (1 Thess. 5.19–22 R.S.V.). The injunction to test everything is translated in the Jerusalem Bible as 'think before you do anything – hold on to what is good'. In modifying the tradition in which I was nurtured I would want to do what the Prayer Book Preface boldly claims has been the wisdom of the Church of England, namely, 'to keep the mean between the two extremes, of too much stiffness in refusing, and too much easiness in admitting any variation from it'. What, then, is the Spirit saying to us in this generation?

First, there is a growing emphasis on what may be called secular holiness, which simply means holiness lived out in the world. We are urged to become involved in the affairs of this world at every level, social, political, as well as religious. 'The kingdom of heaven is like the yeast a woman took and mixed in with three measures of flour till it was leavened all through' (Matt. 13.33). The yeast cannot do its work till it is mixed in with the flour. Christians have been too much inclined to live apart, to try to influence society from outside. In so far as this is true, it has been misguided. Our Lord's work of saving the world involved him in the Incarnation, and complete identification with man. Christians are meant to live life to the full. Such a re-emphasis is positive gain. But there is another side. There are other parables beside that of the yeast. The Christian is a sower of seed, a labourer in the harvest, a fisher of men. Jesus was identified with men, but also separate from them. He often withdrew from the world for fellowship with his Father. If there is danger in being remote from the world, there is danger too in becoming too much like the world. Much of the teaching of Jesus runs clean contrary to the world's ideas, as in the matter of great men making their authority felt. 'This is not to happen among you', he said (Mark 10.43). We are to be in the world, but not of it.

Another way of expressing secular holiness is to say that we are to be world-affirming, not world-denying. This is God's world. He made it, and pronounced it very good (Gen. 1.31). We have to show that we agree with that verdict by accepting from God who, 'out of his riches, gives us all that we need for our happiness' (1 Tim. 6.17). From the creation story we can infer the sanctity of marriage, the dignity of labour, and our stewardship of the material things of the world. But again there is another side. In Genesis the story of creation is followed by the story of the fall. God's good world has become tainted by the sin of man. There is a sense in which the world must be renounced. 'Because the world refused to acknowledge him, therefore it does not acknowledge us' (1 John 3.1). The world, society organized without reference to God, stands over against the Church. So John could say : 'You must not love this passing world or anything that is in the world . . . and the world, with all it craves for, is coming to an end; but anyone who does the will of God remains for ever' (1 John 2.15, 17). Alongside the truth that God gives us all that we need for our happiness we have to place such a saying of our Lord's as : 'None of you can be my disciple unless he give up all his possessions' (Luke 14.33).

Certainly holiness is concerned with this present world, but not at the expense of concern with the world to come. It is truly other-worldly holiness which is most noted for effective service in this world. When Jesus appointed the Twelve, they were to be his companions and to be sent out to preach, with power to cast out devils' (Mark 3.14). Of course there must be the going out to preach and to cast out every kind of evil, but unless there is also conscious companionship with Jesus there will be little power. I recently read an article, urging Christians to become involved in a wide variety of social issues, which concluded : 'But we shan't get very far until we get up off our knees'.* This may be very good advice. But it recognizes the fact that Christians are already on their knees, and I would add that if they are to be effective they will return to the same position. The secular holiness for this age must keep its dimension of eternity if it is not to lose its holiness and become merely secular. When Christian came into the house of the Interpreter he was at the beginning of his journey, a pilgrimage which was to take him right into the world as a soldier of Jesus Christ. The first thing he was shown was 'a Picture of a very grave Person' : 'It had eyes lifted up to Heaven, the best of Books in his hand, the Law of Truth was written upon his lips, the World was behind his back. It stood as if it pleaded with men, and a Crown of Gold did hang over his head'. It is a picture of holiness we cannot ignore, and far removed from 'the escapism and empty echoes of the big meeting or the retreat from reality which often masquerades as personal piety'.† From both these things John Bunyan would have revolted in horror.

A second characteristic of the contemporary scene is the charismatic movement. A great change has come about since Bishop Stephen Neill could write in 1940 : 'I suppose most of us in our work have encountered difficulties caused by some who claim the Pentecostal name, and have been

* *Crusade* editorial, February 1974.
† Ibid.

dismayed to find that the work of those who profess to b
actuated by the Holy Spirit of God, the Spirit of unity
results only in division and confusion in the Churches. W
have here a good example of what has often happened befor
in the history of the Church : when a doctrine which is th
rightful possession of the whole Church is forgotten o
allowed to slip into the background or is not duly em
phasized. God allows it for a time to become embodied ir
a sect, which acts as a gadfly to awaken the Church, unti
the missing doctrine is reabsorbed to the enrichment of th
whole of the common life. The Pentecostal groups do bea
brave and uncompromising witness to one of the funda
mental truths of the revelation of God in Christ, that it i
the will of God that every Christian should consciousl
receive and enjoy the witness and power of the Holy Ghost'.*
The change is not only that Pentecostal groups are no longe
as divisive or exclusive as they once were, and accept, and
are accepted by, Christians of other denominations as fellow
believers; but, more remarkably, that the distinctive
teachings and experiences of Pentecostalism have come to be
treasured by members of every branch of the Church. No
only are there those in all the historic churches who claim
to have been baptized in the Holy Spirit, and exercise
spiritual gifts, including tongues, but there is a new interest
in the person and work of the Holy Spirit on the part of
many who cannot go all the way with Pentecostal teaching.
This surely is positive gain.

I have already expressed some disagreement with the
use of the phrase 'baptism in the Spirit' to indicate a special
experience different from the original initiation into Christ
and his Church. But this does not mean that I think we
should deny the validity of such an experience, or the need
of every Christian to seek at all times to be filled with the
Spirit. Did not Paul remind young Timothy to 'fan into a

* *Beliefs.* The Christian Literature Society for India. 1940. p. 1.

flame the gift that God gave you when I laid hands on you' (2 Tim. 1.6)? God's gift, the following verse tells us, was 'the Spirit of Power, and love, and self-control'. I have also expressed some doubt as to whether the gift of tongues is an essential mark of the blessing of the Holy Spirit. But I would certainly not wish to limit the sovereign power of the Spirit to distribute different gifts to different people just as he chooses (1 Cor. 12.11). In other words, I believe the charismatic movement is a challenge to all Christians to take seriously the words : 'I believe in the Holy Ghost'.

For one thing, we need to recover the sense of the supernatural in daily life, and to know in a vivid way the power and guidance of the Spirit. Yet at the same time it is possible to over-emphasize experience at the expense of doctrine. In the spiritual life there is room for emotion, but feelings alone are a false guide. It is not only in gatherings of a 'pentecostal' kind that emotions can be so stirred as to produce 'results' of a superficial kind, but since in those circles people are taught to anticipate the more exciting gifts, it is probable that the danger in such meetings is greater. It is well known, for instance, that speaking in tongues is a phenomenon not confined to Christianity, and may be induced by any kind of religious excitement. This is by no means to denigrate speaking in tongues, if and when it is a genuine gift of the Spirit, but it does point to the need for caution. The same is true of the liberty and joy so freely expressed by pentecostals. We need it, and it can be a genuine release of spiritual life. But it has its counterfeit in worked up emotion, induced by repetitive singing and gestures, which may lead to disillusionment.

The answer is not to discourage the spontaneity and freedom of expression of those who rejoice in a new-found experience, but to balance it with solid doctrine from the Scriptures. Holiness must be based on the facts of the gospel, apprehended by faith, and not at all dependent on feelings.

The liberty of those who know themselves emancipated from their old inhibitions is not in the least inconsistent with that stern self discipline and obedience to God's laws which the New Testament demands. If a new and vivid experience of the Holy Spirit's power is granted in a moment of revelation, this is all the more a call to continue in the life of the Spirit, growing in grace by ways which may appear quite unspectacular. The fervour of spirit which is often a mark of the Holy Spirit's presence needs to be matched by the tranquillity of a faith which simply trusts the promises of God. It was when J. G. Whittier, the American Quaker, was disturbed by the rowdyism of a revivalist meeting that he wrote the poem which contains the lines –

> Drop thy still dews of quietness,
>   Till all our strivings cease;
> Take from our souls the strain and stress,
> And let our ordered lives confess
>   The beauty of thy peace.

It might be argued that this was simply emotion of another kind, and certainly religious experience of whatever form needs to be tested by the standard of the Bible. A firm intellectual and spiritual grasp of revealed truth is the essential foundation of a holy life. None stressed this more than the Puritans, and renewed interest in their writings has helped to correct the dangers inherent in an excessively experiential religion.

On that note I am content to end these thoughts on the way forward towards a spirituality for the days to come. The Bible portrays a truly secular holiness, the dimension of eternity brought into very human and earthy situations. If we base our religion firmly on the Bible it will always be relevant, always miraculously up-to-date. The Bible is the literature of religious experience, but of experience

94

resulting, not from man's search for God, but from God's self-disclosure, Father, Son and Holy Spirit, three Persons and one God. God is always beckoning us forward : his presence is ever moving. If at times we want to stand still we shall become enmeshed in tradition. If at other times we reach out for novelty we shall find that God is not coming our way, but waiting for us to return to his. The way forward is the way of faith, one step at a time. One of the best-loved hymns of the Keswick Convention sums it up –

> My goal is God Himself, not joy, nor peace,
> Nor even blessing, but Himself, my God ;
> 'Tis His to lead me there – not mine, but His –
> At any cost, dear Lord, by any road.

> So faith bounds forward to its goal in God,
> And love can trust her Lord to lead her there ;
> Upheld by Him, my soul is following hard
> Till God hath full fulfilled my deepest prayer.

> No matter if the way be sometimes dark,
> Not matter though the cost be oft-times great,
> He knoweth how I best shall reach the mark,
> The way that leads to Him must needs be strait.

> One thing I know, I cannot say Him nay ;
> One thing I do, I press towards my Lord ;
> My God my glory here, from day to day,
> And in the glory there my great Reward.

F. Brook

Books for Further Reading

Stephen Neill, *Christian Holiness* (Lutterworth Press, 1960).

J. C. Ryle, *Holiness* (Inter-Varsity Press, 1962).

Donald Bridge and David Phypers, *Spiritual gifts and the Church* (Inter-Varsity Press, 1973).

Kenneth Prior, *The Way of Holiness* (Inter-Varsity Press, 1967).

Michael Green, *New life, New lifestyle* (Hodder & Stoughton, 1973).

W. E. Sangster, *The Path to Perfection* (Hodder & Stoughton, 1943).

The Keswick Week, Verbatim Reports of the Addresses at the Keswick Convention Published annually (Marshall, Morgan and Scott).

J. Oswald Sanders, *Problems of Christian Discipleship* (Lutterworth Press).

A. M. Stibbs and J. I. Packer, *The Spirit Within You* (Hodder & Stoughton, 1967).

J. C. P. Cockerton, *To Be Sure* (Hodder & Stoughton, 1967).